Basics Of Radio Control Sailplanes

by Alan Gornick Jr.

About the Author

Alan Gornick Jr.

Born in New York and raised in Michigan, Alan Gornick Jr. began to build and fly model gliders, as well as rubber-band-powered free-flight and scale models, while still in elementary school. As his age and skills increased, so did the complexity of the models that he built and flew. U-control combat planes provided vast amounts of building experience (and scrap materials), while U-control stunts provided valuable flying experience.

On completing college, Alan moved to Los Angeles, where he had the good fortune to live near an outstanding slope-soaring site. Soon, both he and his three children were heavily involved in radio-control gliders, and Alan's building activities supplied the material for many of the Field and Bench Reviews published in *Model Airplane News.*

Alan's interest in aviation also extends to the realm of full-scale aviation. He has a commercial pilot's license with an instrument rating, and he's the proud owner of a 250hp Starduster Too open-cockpit biplane, which he flies in aerobatic competition and "just for the pure joy of it." He's currently president of the Los Angeles chapter of the International Aerobatic Club.

Alan is a director of photography in the theatrical motion-picture industry, as well as a freelance writer and photographer.

Publisher: Louis DeFrancesco, Jr.
Editor: Rich Uravitch
Book Design: Mary Lou Ramos
Cover Design: Alan Palermo
Copy Editors: Lynne Sewell, Katherine Tolliver
Cover Photography: Alan Gornick, Jr., John Lupperger
Cover Illustration: Alan Gornick, Jr.
Line Illustrations: Alan Gornick III

Contents

Introduction

This is a book about having fun with radio-control gliders and sailplanes, with the primary emphasis on *having fun!* And make no mistake about it, flying R/C gliders and sailplanes is *fun!*

On the premise that activities are more enjoyable when we're successful at them than when we're not, this book is written with the intention of providing you with all the information needed for successful, enjoyable flying, regardless of your present skill level. Whether you're just starting out, are already an accomplished pilot flying for the pure joy of it, or enjoy flying in competition, you'll find plenty of information here to assist and challenge you in your pursuit of this fascinating sport and hobby.

This book is structured in such a manner that each chapter stands alone, although almost everyone will find an initial cover-to-cover reading beneficial. Additionally, cross-references have been provided in the text to indicate where pertinent information in other chapters and sections can be found. The companies and organizations mentioned are listed alphabetically at the end of the book.

I hope this book helps you to get as much pleasure out of your flying as I have been privileged to enjoy while gaining the experience required to write it. Have fun!

Choosing the Model

Basic Multi-Purpose Gliders

If this is your first model glider, your choice is simple: Acquire an uncomplicated, inexpensive 2-meter glider with a polyhedral wing and two-axis rudder/elevator controls. "Whazzat?" you ask; "What does that mean?"

Open-class glider in flight.

Well, 2-meter refers to the wingspan, and in this case, it's 78³/4 inches or less from wing tip to wing tip. I've chosen this size because it's easy to build, easily transportable, and easy to launch with minimal equipment.

Now refer to Fig.1-1. That slight bend at the center of the wing is called "dihedral," and it causes the airplane to turn when we apply sideways pressure on the rudder stick. The additional bend near the tip of each wing is called "polyhedral." Polyhedral also helps our glider to turn but, more important, it helps to stabilize it so that, when properly set up, it will recover from mistakes and unusual attitudes all by itself! Needless to say, this is a most desirable characteristic in a first airplane, and you can be sure you'll use it to full advantage when you first learn to fly!

As for the rudder/elevator specification, all we really need to control our glider's pitch (up/down) angle and direction are two controls: The elevator controls pitch, while the rudder, in combination with polyhedral, rolls the wings into, and out of, banks for turns. As you'll learn in a later chapter, these simple controls will even allow us to perform many aerobatic maneuvers, including loops, barrel rolls, snap rolls and spins!

Gliders possessing the aforementioned characteristics can be used for both thermal flying and slope flying. They fly slowly enough to allow the novice pilot plenty of time to learn correct control inputs, recover from errors and develop the reflexive hand/eye coordination that's crucial to successfully flying faster, more complicated aircraft. These gliders are also light, compact and easy to transport; they can be hand-launched for slope flying, or launched with the aid of a hi-start, a winch, a hand tow, or a

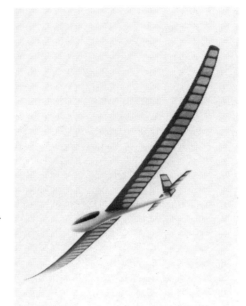

Bob Martin Models Hobie Hawk

power pod for thermal flying. Another advantage that might not be immediately apparent, but will be greatly appreciated soon enough, is that a glider's mass is sufficiently small for any impact damage to be minimal! In addition to learning and fun-flying, if your skills and interests lead you toward thermal contest flying, you'll find a category set up specifically for the 2-meter glider. These are true, all-purpose airplanes providing many years of fun!

A primary consideration regarding the choice of a first glider is whether it should be ready-made (custom-built), almost-ready-to-fly (also known as an ARF), self-built from a kit, or scratch-built from plans. I think the beginner glider pilot is far better off building from a kit, because crashes and the resultant damage are

piece; instead, make it simple and strong. More information on this will be found in the chapter on building techniques.

Some excellent choices in the 2-meter kit category are Carl Goldberg's Gentle Lady, House of Balsa's 2x4, Bob Martin R/C Models' Pussycat, Airtronics' Olympic 650, Top Flite's Metrick and the Craft Air Drifter II. These are easy-to-build kits featuring clear instructions writ-

glider will allow you to be airborne in just a few hours after carting the package home. This is an excellent 2-meter design with over 90 percent of the work already done for you.

Basic Slope Gliders

Even though you might be an accomplished thermal soaring pilot, for your first slope-flying experiences, I strongly recommend the use of a basic 2-meter polyhedral glider as described in the previous section. Why? Because even the slowest and most forgiving of the gliders designed specifically for slope soaring flies and lands (and crashes!) at much higher speeds than a 2-meter design; it takes a seasoned pilot to stay ahead of these babies! Further, they also lack

Cal-Soar tipperon-equipped Accipiter

Carl Goldberg Models Gentle Lady

Bob Martin Models Katie II

a normal and inevitable part of learning to fly. Naturally, a modeler who initially built the glider will be in a far better position to repair it than one who bought a ready-made plane or an ARF. Similarly, it would be a shame to spend considerable time on scratch-building, only to smash all your handiwork to smithereens on the first flight! Don't spend too much time making your first glider a show-

ten with beginners in mind. The careful builder of any of these kits (if you're a novice, see the chapter entitled "Building Techniques") will be rewarded with an excellent multi-purpose glider that's capable of providing many years of flying enjoyment.

If you simply don't have the time to assemble your own glider from a kit, Hobby Shack's EZ-2000 ARF

the inherent stability and self-righting characteristics of 2-meter polyhedral gliders. It's much easier to learn the mechanics of slope lift, sink and landings with a 2-meter floater than with a slope glider.

Assuming that you've mastered the slopes with your 2-meter glider, let's look at gliders designed specifically for slope flying. For your first slope glider, I recommend a straight-wing

Bob Martin Models SR-7

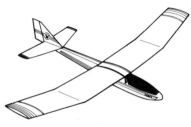

Eagle II

Top Flite Models Metrick

type with a flat-bottom airfoil and two-axis aileron/elevator controls, (preferably one with a tough fuselage, as most slope sites have pretty rugged landing areas). The flat-bottom airfoil will provide plenty of lift (it will even allow aerobatic flights of reasonable duration from a hi-start!), while aileron control will provide

crisp roll response for turns and aerobatics.

One good example of this type of glider is the Bob Martin R/C Models Katie II, which has a 72-inch balsa-sheeted foam wing and a fuselage made of Duralene, which is a synthetic material that's guaranteed by its manufacturer to be unbreakable. That claim is fairly accurate, by the way—as I found out when I tried to move a house with my first Katie II (yes, I still have it!). Neither the house nor the fuselage broke, although the wing sure did! Two days later, the Katie was back in the air as

good as new. As slope gliders go, the Katie II is a relatively slow-flying, forgiving airplane, but it's also capable of performing some pretty awesome aerobatics, and it penetrates well in strong winds. You can even thermal with the thing! It's an excellent choice for a basic slope trainer.

Fig. 1-1: Typical 2-meter glider showing polyhedral.

Intermediate and Advanced Slope Gliders

When you've mastered the basic two-axis flat-bottom airfoil slope gliders (as outlined in the previous section), move on to gliders with semi-symmetrical or fully symmetrical airfoils, as these have vastly superior inverted-flight capability. It's important to note that a glider with a semi-symmetrical or symmetrical airfoil has to fly faster than one with a flat-bottom or under-cambered airfoil to generate the same amount of lift. Be sure your flying skills are such that you'll be

able to keep ahead of your new glider! Eventually, if the ultimate in aerobatic performance is your goal, you'll want a glider that provides control of all three axes: pitch, roll and yaw.

There are innumerable intermediate and advanced slope gliders, and choosing just one can be difficult. Hoping to make that choice simpler for you, I'll try to divide them into categories.

Intermediate Two-Axis Gliders

In the ARF category, Hobby Shack fills the need once again with its EZ Slope Arrowhead, which is a two-axis glider that's easily expandable to three axes when you're ready. One of the most durable intermediate gliders providing excellent performance is Bob Martin R/C Models' Coyote, which features a Duralene fuselage and looks a lot like a jet fighter. The Coyote has an exceptionally wide speed range, making it one of the most versatile aircraft in this category. Perhaps the most long-lived, and certainly one of the fastest, intermediate/advanced slope glider is the Pierce Aero Ridge Rat. The roll rate on this little 49-inch-wingspan devil is pretty awesome when it's built according to the plans; you can imagine what it (and its minimum air speed) became when one of my buddies produced a clip-wing version by lopping three bays off each wing!

Top Flite Models Wristocrat hand-launch

Top Flite Antares - F3B

Bob Martin Models Talon

High-Performance Two-Axis Gliders

We're fortunate to have two exceptional aircraft featuring Duralene fuselages in this category and both look like high-performance jet fighter/interceptors: Larry Hargrave's beautiful Jaguar, and Bob Martin R/C Models' sleek, fast SR-7. The Jaguar successfully spans the intermediate to expert categories; it handles a wide range of air speeds from moderately fast to very fast, and it's an exciting, versatile aerobatic performer. The SR-7 is an expert's airplane—the one you haul out when the wind's howling and sane people are indoors. At those times, nothing is as exhilarating as flying an SR-7. It can certainly be flown successfully in more moderate conditions, but it's really designed to handle the rough stuff. When landing under such conditions, that guarantee of "unbreakability" is most comforting!

Hand-Launch Gliders

Other great high-performance two-axis gliders are the lightweight hand-launched types. These are especially well-suited to small flying areas, or times when you just feel like flying in close. Because of their lightness, they fly best in light to moderate winds. One of my favorites is the scratch-built Acro-Zephyr designed by Bob

Owens. This little zipper even features an index-finger-size compartment in the bottom of the fuselage to expedite land-launching! Of the kit-built lightweights, the ingeniously

Launching a basic 2-meter glider.

designed and streamlined Talon, manufactured by Bob Martin R/C Models, is an excellent choice. The Talon can be built with either a conventional tail or a V-tail. Another

intriguing and speedy lightweight is Combat Models' all-foam F-16 slope soarer. As an additional advantage, any of the lightweight hand-launch gliders will fit into even a compact

car when fully assembled; this means no more forgotten wing bolts or rubber bands to keep us from flying!

Flying Wings

Some of the most versatile and interesting types of two-axis slope gliders are the flying wings. I have a highly modified version of the Gryphon, which has fully symmetrical wings and is a fantastic aerobatic performer. Because of its symmetrical airfoil, it flies as well inverted as it does upright. It can easily fly chained outside maneuvers, turning on a dime and giving back change, and then climb away, and even thermal, inverted! For those of you who like to think and fly big, consider Hobby Lobby's

Launching open-class glider

Multiplex's Cortina. It has a 137-inch wingspan, pre-built foam wings sheeted with obechi wood, and a fiberglass fuselage.

Three-Axis Gliders

Some aerobatic maneuvers are difficult or impossible without rudder control; hammerheads and snap rolls are a couple of examples. For the ultimate in aerobatic performance, the three-axis glider is the answer. It

enables the pilot to position it in many attitudes by using elevator, rudder and ailerons. In setting up the radio-control functions for three-axis flight, it's customary to put elevator and ailerons on the right stick, and the rudder on the left stick. This is referred to as Mode II.

An excellent choice in this category is the Askant, kitted by Aeronautics, Inc. The Askant has a fiberglass fuselage and sheeted-foam wings with built-in ballast tubes. For those in a hurry to fly, Hobby Shack's EZ Arrowhead can be flown with elevator and aileron while learning, and the rudder can be added

when the pilot is ready to go all-out. Robbe's scale-like Verso is larger and a great performer. Its 82-inch obechi-sheeted foam wings carry around a heavy-duty shock-absorbing plastic fuselage. The Verso flies best at large flying sites with moderate to high winds. Craft Air's T-tailed Freedom is another top aerobatic performer. It's especially appreciated at sites with rocks or trash in the landing area, because it's more likely to remain with the glider when encoun-

tering such obstacles. Sometimes, we need all the help we can get!

If you're looking for something really different, the Accipter CCT from California Soaring Products may be just the ticket. In addition to rudder, stabilator, and flaps with a range of 6 degrees positive to 80 degrees negative, the Accipter CCT uses tipperons for roll control. What's a tipperon? Hack off the outboard 8 inches or so of each wing, then rejoin it to the inboard section in such a way that it can be rotated about the thickest part of the wing's cross section. Presto! You have a tipperon! Rotating the tipperons changes their angle of attack, thus causing the glider to roll.

Intermediate and Advanced Thermal Gliders

This category generally includes gliders of more specialized design and/or construction than the multipurpose models: gliders with wingspans greater than 2 meters, or those with control functions beyond the basic ones of elevator and rudder. Beyond that, the design purpose of many, if not most, of the gliders in this category is to win in thermal glider competition. For that reason, I'll discuss them according to their competition classes.

Two-Meter Class. As I've already discussed, this class is for gliders with a wingspan of 2 meters (78$\frac{3}{4}$ inches) or less. While the 2-meter gliders discussed in the Basic Multipurpose Glider section of this chapter are all fine choices for thermal contests and sport flying, a few gliders, by virtue of their design and/or construction, rightfully belong in the intermediate and advanced categories.

One such glider is Airtronics' sleek Sagitta 600, which has a slender (read "fragile"), streamlined (lots of sanding) fuselage that has slightly less drag than many other designs. If you want, the Sagitta's wing can be fitted for spoilers (for contests, it is), and the plane is a proven top performer. Another top-performing glider is Dynaflite's Mini-Bird of Time that features an unusual and complex wing planform that you can build either 8.5 percent (faster) or 11 percent (more lift and slower) thick.

An interesting three-axis glider is the Prodigy from Off The Ground Models. It features carbon-fiber-reinforced spruce spars, which stand up to pilots enamored of lead-foot electric-winch launches with zoom releases. Another fine 2-meter glider that adds flaps to its three-axis controls is the Prophet from Davey Systems Corporation.

Finally—and just for the fun of it—the lightweight hand-launch gliders pack a lot of flying enjoyment into their small airframes and into a small airspace as well. Some good ones are Top Flite's neat little Wristocrat, which comes with a free-flight junior partner, and the scratch-built Zephyr, designed by Bob Owens. Off The Ground Models' Tantrum is a really intriguing design; weighing only 10 ounces, it can be built with folding outer wing panels, and its total wingspan is 42 inches. A couple of other lightweights oriented more to competition (Class A, for gliders 1^1/2 meters or less) are the Ariel, kitted by Davey Systems Corporation, and the Gnome from Midway Model Company.

Standard Class. Gliders with a wingspan of 100 inches or less fall into the standard class. Airtronics' Olympic II is a classic standard-class glider that's well-suited to beginners, yet fully competitive. It's easy to build, docile to fly, and performs very well. The same can also be said for Dynaflite's Windrifter and Sig's Riser 100. Also available from Airtronics is the Cumic Plus, which features a tough fiberglass fuselage.

Moving into more complex and competition-oriented gliders, there's the beautiful El Primero Grande from Buzz Waltz R/C Designs and, of course, Airtronics' sleek Sagitta 900. Because of its complicated construction and speedy flight characteristics, the Sagitta is recommended only for experienced builders and fliers. For

experienced pilots who want a beautiful high-tech glider for both thermal and slope soaring, the Hobie Hawk from Bob Martin R/C Models is a terrific choice; I have three, and I love them!

Open Class. The open class comprises gliders with wingspans of over 100 inches, and is totally unrestricted in the number of controls allowed. Most of the gliders available in this class are very complicated, both in design and operation, and most have wingspans of over 10 feet. These big expensive aircraft require skill to build and fly, and while they can also be a lot of fun, I really can't recommend them for pleasurable Sunday cruising. For that purpose, I'd rather crash something cheaper and easier to repair! They do, however, offer an irresistible challenge for the competition-oriented.

Buzz Waltz R/C Designs offers its 118-inch wingspan Con Quistador, and what a wing it has! It features a complex built-up construction that begs to be covered in transparent MonoKote. Among the classics are the Pierce Aero Paragon, Larry Jolly's Pantera, and Dynaflite's Mirage and Bird of Time. If you really like your gliders BIG, Craft Air's Sailaire has a 149-inch wingspan and is a delightful slow floater with excellent flight characteristics. Even bigger is the Pierce Aero Paramount, which has a 156-inch wingspan; it, too, flies well and boasts a wide speed range.

For those of you who like lots of control functions, Dodgson Designs' Camano and Windsong should provide all the thumb and finger twiddling you want. Both have flaps and spoilers, as well as the usual three-axis controls. My favorite is Airtronics' Adante, which is a three-axis glider with spoilers and full-span flaperons capable of both reflex and positive extension. The Adante has an exceptionally wide speed range and exhibits smooth, positive flight characteristics. Of course, you'll need a 5-channel radio to complement any of these aircraft.

Hobby Lobby/Graupner Discus

F3B Multi-task Gliders. Gliders used in F3B competition must be capable of performing three tasks well: thermal duration, speed and distance. Obviously, their designs make a number of compromises, but they're compromises that make them excellent all-around aircraft.

For those who may be considering F3B (multi-task) competition, Bob Martin R/C Models' three-axis Bobcat fills the bill at a minimal cost while providing slope aerobatic thrills, too. Another excellent choice is the 100-inch-wingspan Gemini MTS kitted by Pierce Aero; it can also be flown successfully in the standard class. Top Flite's Antares, with a 99^3/4-inch wingspan, adds flaps to its three-axis design for top all-around performance in thermals and on the slope, as well as for F3B competition.

Scale Sailplanes

An R/C scale sailplane gracefully gliding across the sky is certainly a beautiful sight, and it provides a great deal of pleasure for the skilled pilot. Notice, I said "skilled." The reason for this is that scale sailplanes fly very much like their full-scale counterparts and are subject to the same operating limitations. If you pull or push too many Gs, whether in aerobatic flight or not, the glider will break. If the full-size glider has nasty characteristics (e.g., tip-stalling), the scale model will, too. This means that to be flown successfully, they must be flown in a scale-like way. Forget this, and your only consolation might be that you weren't in the plane when *that* happened!

Very few scale sailplanes are made in the United States; almost all are imported from Europe. They're usually beautifully crafted and kitted, and usually expensive. If the quality doesn't bring a tear to your eye, the price certainly will; but to enthusiasts, they're worth every penny.

Two excellent U.S.-made scale sailplanes are Astro Flight's two-axis, 100-inch wingspan ASW-15, and its three-axis, 132-inch wingspan ASW-17. American Sailplane Designs offers a 1/3-scale ASW-20 with a fiberglass fuselage, a 4.5-meter LS-3, a 4-meter ASW-17, and a 3.8- to 4.4-meter fully aerobatic Salto. The last three feature gel-coated fuselages and obechi-skinned foam wings and tails.

Of the European manufacturers, Graupner, Aviomodelli, Robbe, Krick, Cirrus, Wik Modelle, Multiplex, and many others produce high-quality scale models of just about any full-scale glider ever flown, and they also produce many non-scale models of their own (but I certainly don't have enough room to review them here!). Of special interest are Krick's 1/5-scale, 1936 Minimoa; two sizes of the 1932 Grunau Baby; a 1/6-scale 1937-39 Reiher; and a 1/4-scale 1938 Schulgleiter SG-38! Any of these are guaranteed to attract lots of attention at your flying site! The Krick models are all manufactured to exact scale and are available from Hobby Lobby.

Hobby Lobby/Graupner ASW-22

The Choice is Yours

As you can see, there's an available glider design for just about any type of flying and in almost any stage of completion. Again, don't be tempted to buy a model with all the bells and whistles when you're starting; you'll just end up with a box full of expensive scrap! Instead, buy an inexpensive, but forgiving, 2-meter "floater"; learn to fly (and repair) it well; then move up gradually in glider complexity and capability as you focus on the type of soaring that most appeals to you.

Your Glider's Controls

I don't want to get into a lengthy discussion of aerodynamic theory here; after all, this is supposed to be a book about the *fun* of flying. However, a basic understanding of how gliders and their controls function and how those controls are used, will assist you in evaluating and obtaining peak performance from the gliders you choose and fly, and that's fun! (Fig. 2-1 shows a full-house 5-channel glider.)

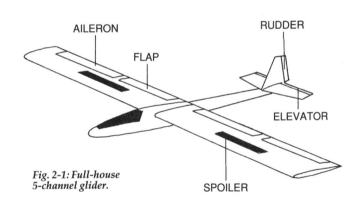

Fig. 2-1: Full-house 5-channel glider.

AILERON
FLAP
RUDDER
ELEVATOR
SPOILER

Wings, Lift, and Performance

By carefully choosing the airfoil of your glider's wing and utilizing it appropriately, you can control the manner in which it develops lift and, thereby, its in-flight performance. Let's take a look at how a wing develops lift.

Generation of Lift. Figure 2-2 depicts a flat-bottomed type of airfoil and the airflow around it. As you can see, because of the wing's curvature, air passing over the top of the wing must travel farther than air flowing past the bottom of the wing. Since the wing is moving through the air at a constant speed, it follows that the

air on top must move faster than that on the bottom and thus, according to Bernoulli's Principle and simple logic, must be less dense and possess lower pressure than that on the bottom. It's this lower pressure at the top of the wing that creates lift. As the angle of attack (the angle of the wing's chord line relative to the wind) is increased, a lifting force is also generated by the force of the wind against the bottom of the wing (Fig. 2-3). However, this lifting force is at best just a small part (less than 25 percent) of the total lift generated by the wing. You can prove this by sticking your hand out the window of a moving car: First, hold your hand flat in the airflow and vary the angle of attack, then do the same thing with your hand cupped in the shape of an airfoil. Do this at varying speeds also. I'll wait until you come back...

You probably noticed that as you increased the angle of attack of your hand against the wind, the lift also increased until a point was reached where your hand no longer generated lift. As you approached this point, you could feel a buffeting on the back of your hand as the airflow started to separate from the airfoil (your hand), then, as you increased the angle of attack still further, your hand was abruptly blown backward as it lost lift totally. That phenomenon is known as a stall, and the same thing happens to airplanes when their wing's angle of attack exceeds what is termed the critical angle of attack.

A logical conclusion from the above is that, for any given airfoil, lift can only be increased by increasing the speed, and/or the angle of attack (to the critical angle), of our glider's wing through the air.

Four Forces. Our glider is acted upon by four forces in flight: lift,

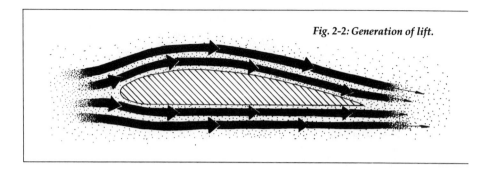

Fig. 2-2: Generation of lift.

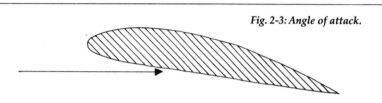

Fig. 2-3: Angle of attack.

gravity, thrust, and drag. In stabilized flight, lift balances gravity, and thrust balances drag (Fig. 2-4). Since gliders have no engines, they depend on gravity and/or stored inertia to develop the thrust that moves the airfoil forward. Thus, in still air and in stabilized flight, gliders are always sinking relative to the air surrounding them, because these four forces cannot balance each other in any other manner. From the above, you can see why light weight and low drag are such important factors in glider design and construction.

Airfoil Design. Another factor that greatly affects glider performance is airfoil shape, which directly affects lift. There are an infinite number of possible airfoil shapes, and catalogs

and books about them go on ad nauseam. While there are refinements, for our purposes we can narrow the field to three basic types: for maximum lift at low air speeds, undercambered (camber is the degree of curvature in a wing's surface) or flat-bottomed airfoils are generally best; for a compromise between lift and maneuverability at slightly higher air speeds, I would probably choose a semi-symmetrical airfoil; and for all-out aerobatic performance at necessarily high air speeds, nothing beats a fully-symmetrical airfoil. Now I'll commit blasphemy among the technically oriented who thrive upon minutiae by telling you that, within these broad categories and in the real world, pilot ability is far more impor-

tant in determining aircraft performance than subtle differences in airfoil design. Choose the airfoil type best suited to your needs and learn to fly it well—the competition will melt in your slipstream!

Three Primary Axes of Flight

An axis is defined as a line passing through a body's center of rotation, and an airplane's center of rotation will always be located at its center of gravity. Through the use of our glider's controls, we can cause it to rotate about one or more of three primary axes (Fig. 2-5).

Pitch. Movement of the elevator, or stabilator in some gliders, causes the glider to rotate about its lateral axis, resulting in a change in pitch (nose up or down) attitude. Changing the pitch attitude of the glider allows control of its speed and altitude.

Yaw. Movement of the rudder causes the glider to rotate about its vertical axis, resulting in a yawing motion and change in direction.

Roll. Movement of the ailerons causes the glider to rotate about its longitudinal axis, resulting in a rolling motion. To effect this rolling motion, the aileron on one wing is deflected upward, decreasing that wing's lift, while that on the other is deflected downward, increasing that wing's lift. However, increasing lift also increases drag, result-

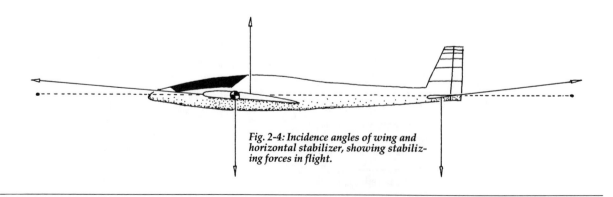

Fig. 2-4: Incidence angles of wing and horizontal stabilizer, showing stabilizing forces in flight.

ing in the glider's yawing in the direction of the wing with the lowered aileron. This effect is termed adverse yaw, and can only be compensated for by use of the rudder. This is why full three-axis controls are preferred by those flying advanced thermal and aerobatic gliders.

Spoilers

Why in the world would we want to decrease lift? A few reasons are to escape a strong thermal, to shorten the glide for a precise spot landing, or to increase the glider's rate of descent without exceeding a safe air speed. All of these goals can be accomplished through the use of spoilers. Spoilers are panels that can be extended above the surface of the wing, reducing the wing's lift by disrupting the smooth flow of air across it. It doesn't take a very large spoiler to greatly affect the lift-producing capability of a wing (Fig. 2-6).

Flaps

Flaps are moveable panels at the trailing edge of the wing that can be deflected downward, and in some cases upward, to change the camber of the glider's wing. When deflected downward, they increase both lift and drag, enabling the glider to make steeper landing approaches (perhaps to clear trees) at lower air speeds than would be possible without them. When deflected upward (called reflex flap), the wing's lift and drag are both decreased, allowing the glider to travel at higher speeds than it could without this feature. This is very useful for rapidly moving from one thermal to another, or when seeking thermals amongst known lift-producing areas. Some gliders, such as Airtronics' Adante, feature full-span flaperons that function as both flaps and ailerons. These allow continuous control of the wing's camber for optimum performance under a wide range of conditions.

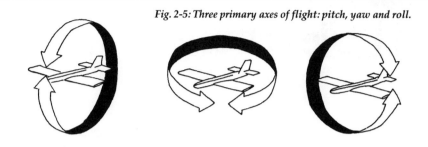

Fig. 2-5: Three primary axes of flight: pitch, yaw and roll.

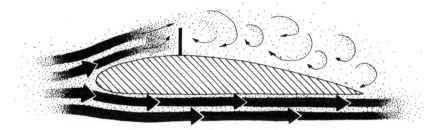

Fig. 2-6: Spoilers showing airflow disruption.

Choosing A Radio

Choosing a proper radio can be perplexing, both for first-time buyers and experienced enthusiasts. The choice is made even more complicated by the changing FCC (Federal Communications Commission) regulations and frequency assignments for R/C applications. These should all be fully implemented by January 1, 1991, but things could be pretty confusing in the interim. For the moment, let's concentrate on choosing the best radio for your application, moving on to frequency selection and the technical details a little later.

A 2-stick Mode I radio.

Your First Radio

While your first glider will only require two channels (rudder and elevator), I strongly recommend that you purchase at least a 4-channel radio. You'll eventually want to move on to more sophisticated gliders with more control functions, and a 4-channel radio will allow this future expansion. Also, the preferred method of setting up aircraft controls is with the elevator and primary turn control (rudder or ailerons, depending on the aircraft design) on the right stick, and secondary controls on the left stick. This is known as Mode II. Typical secondary controls for a glider with aileron/elevator primary controls would add rudder to the left stick, with the possible addition of spoilers, flaps, tow-hook release, etc. Finally, the price differential between a 2-channel and a 4-channel system is relatively insignificant, so you might as well buy the more flexible and, therefore, more usable radio.

One final consideration when buying a radio is to make sure that both transmitter and receiver batteries are of the nickel-cadmium (Ni-Cd) variety, because they're infinitely more reliable and, being rechargeable, far less expensive in the long run than alkaline or carbon/zinc batteries, which have to be replaced. Non-rechargeable batteries are obsolete; shun them!

Radio Modes

There are three major modes of aircraft radio operation: Mode I, Mode II and Single Stick (Fig. 3-1.)

Mode I places the primary pitch control (elevator) on the right stick, with the primary turn control (either rudder or aileron, depending on aircraft design) on the left stick. In my opinion, this mode is awkward and confusing, and it requires two thumbs to do what should be the work of one. Unfortunately, most 2-channel radios are configured for Mode I operation, and a beginner buying such a radio will have great difficulty finding someone to help with those crucial first flights, as almost no one flies using Mode I, so forget it!

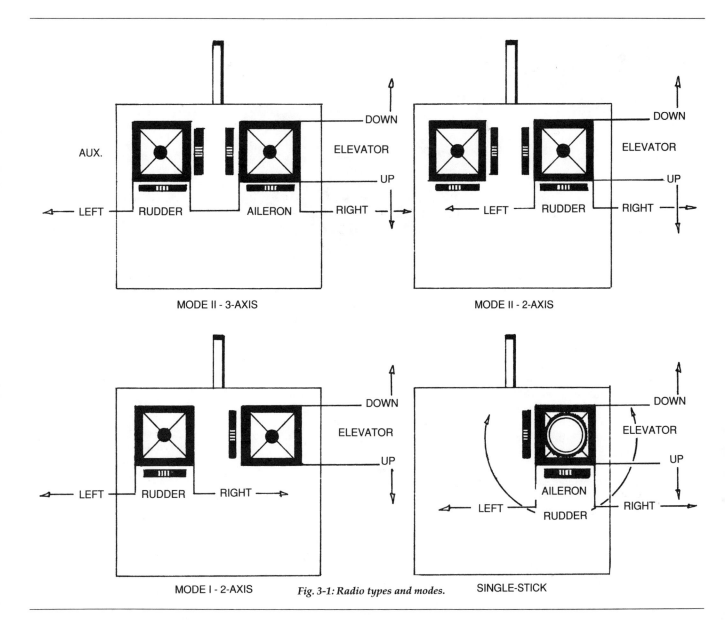

Fig. 3-1: Radio types and modes.

Mode II places both primary controls (elevator/rudder, or elevator/aileron for 2-channel gliders) on the right stick, and secondary controls are assigned to the left stick and/or additional switches. Thus, a 3-channel glider would be set up with elevator and aileron on the right stick and rudder on the left stick. This is a much more instinctive means of control than Mode I, and most people will learn far more readily using a Mode II configuration than with any other.

Single-stick radios place three controls on the right stick: elevator and aileron are respectively controlled by fore/aft and right/left movements of the stick, while the rudder is controlled by rotating a large knob on top of the stick. This requires that the stick be grasped by the fingers, and this restricts full, smooth movement of the controls and results in a cramped, awkward hand position and a consequently jerky flight. Most fliers find it far easier to put the balls of their thumbs on top of the sticks, thus allowing full freedom of movement and more positive, instinctive control (as in Mode II). Some pilots, however, love single stick, and if you're one of them, enjoy, and fly in peace!

Radio Features

Radios are no different from most consumer goods, and the R/C modeler is blessed with a full line of radio products, from the most basic to almost automatic, from which to choose. Fortunately for our wallets, the most sophisticated (read "expensive") radios are designed for helicopters and powered, aerobatic, pattern airplanes, and they have features we glider pilots neither want nor need. In many cases, the simpler radios are our wisest choice.

The following is a list of available radio features and their functions:

A basic 4-channel Mode II radio.

● **Trim Control.** These are the sliding potentiometers (pots) located next to the control sticks. They're moved in the direction of desired control travel in order to correct for slight control or balance mis-adjustments, or to trim (configure) the glider for a particular flying speed or situation.

● **Neck Strap.** To the best of my knowledge, every aircraft radio available today is sold equipped with a neck strap, and this should be used at all times while flying. Not only do they prevent you from dropping and damaging your radio with resultant damage and loss of control (not to mention embarrassment), but they also permit easier launching and retrieval.

● **Battery Charge Meter.** This isn't an option; it's a necessity! Since these are invariably mounted on the transmitter, the wise buyer will make sure the airborne receiver battery can be ground-checked with this meter as well. Be aware that Ni-Cd batteries deliver almost full voltage until nearly exhausted, then drop off rapidly; so keep an eye on that meter, and land as soon as it shows less than a full charge. Some transmitter meters, however, measure RF signal strength coming off the antenna, rather than battery status. Check to determine which function your meter is performing.

● **Trainer System.** Many radios have sockets by which two transmitters may be coupled to control one airplane with a cable. Thus, a student pilot can gain experience rapidly, while an instructor monitors the flight. The instructor can take control as soon as the beginner makes a mistake, or he can demonstrate maneuvers. This is a great feature!

● **Dual Rates.** This allows switching between full servo throw and partial servo throw, with the partial throw being a fixed rate of 50 percent in some radios, and adjustable from 30 percent to 100 percent in others. This is handy for gliders with wide speed envelopes, since the faster a plane flies, the more sensitive its controls will become. It's also helpful for gliders set up with huge control throws for aerobatics, allowing easy cruising on low rate, while permitting full performance using high rate.

● **Dual Rate Exponential.** In addition to providing full dual-rate function, this feature permits selection of either linear or exponential response for the low-rate setting. Linear response means that if we move the stick 30 percent, the servo moves in direct proportion, i.e., 30 percent. Exponential response means that over the initial portion of stick travel, the servo will move less than linearly, and over the final portion of stick travel, the servo will move more than linearly. The degree of exponential can be adjusted from very pronounced to none. At all times, the exponential setting allows 100-percent servo throws. This is a fantastic feature for all high-performance airplanes!

● **Servo-Reversing.** A flip of a switch reverses servo direction, allowing any servo to be used for right or left control functions and greatly simplifying radio installation. A word of warning though: If you use the same transmitter for more than one airplane, be sure to check very thoroughly for proper control throws before flying. It's all too easy to get these confused when switching airplanes, and while *you* might be able to cope with the unexpected control reversal, I know *I* can't!

● **End-Point Adjustment.** This allows you to limit the servo travel on one or both sides of center. Not only does this make control adjustment much easier, but it also allows differential aileron or elevon throws, 10-percent reflex versus 40-percent down flaps, etc.

● **Direct Servo Coupling.** With this feature, the transmitter and receiver can be directly connected with a cable, allowing adjustment of controls and trims without transmitting a radio signal. While useful for initial setup, I advise against its use at the field while someone is flying on the same frequency. (I sure wouldn't want to try to convince another pilot that his crash *wasn't* caused by my fiddling with my transmitter!)

● **Coupling Switches.** These are most commonly used for coupling rudder and ailerons for easily coordinated turns. Use of the rudder control will override the coupling feature. Other uses are for elevons on flying wings, flaperons, flap/elevator and spoiler/elevator coupling. Depending on the type and complexity of your glider, this can be an extremely useful feature.

● **Modules.** Frequency modules allow easy, accurate changing between bands and frequencies. They're rather expensive and useful primarily for modelers who travel to a variety of sites that might be affected by local radio interference, or for those days when everyone arriving at the flying site is on the same frequency.

They're also used by sky hogs at heavily used flying sites, but you aren't one of those, are you?

Radio Types

At present, there are three main types of radio-control systems:
- AM (amplitude modulation
- FM (frequency modulation)
- PCM (pulse coded modulation)

Actually, PCM systems are FM radios utilizing special encoding techniques to enhance transmitter/ receiver selectivity and coupling, so it could be argued that there are really only *two* basic types of radio systems: AM and FM.

Which Type of Radio is Best?

To answer this question, we first have to define the intended use: in our case, flying model gliders. Since this is a book about flying, rather than radio-electronic technology, I'll leave the technical gobbledygook to those who thrive on such minutiae and concentrate, instead, on the practical aspects of choosing a radio.

Put simply, if you're interested in entering contests with powered aircraft, PCM is probably your best choice; if you're flying model helicopters, you'll probably opt for FM; but for flying model gliders, it doesn't make any difference which you choose! However, I recommend AM radios, because they're generally less expensive than other types, but any radio offered by a major manufacturer will prove fully satisfactory for flying model gliders. I've flown with AM radios for years (frequently from a slope site smack in the middle of Los Angeles, CA, and in direct line of sight of dozens of radio and

TV antennas), and I've never experienced or observed radio interference that couldn't be traced to someone in the immediate vicinity. That doesn't mean that it can't happen, but I sure don't lose any sleep over it! As long as you choose a radio with the features you require and/or desire, and it's made by a reputable manufacturer, you'll be perfectly satisfied with it, regardless of its type of modulation.

Frequencies (72MHz band)

Presently, the system of radio-frequency allocation, as well as the number of frequencies available, is undergoing major changes. These changes are being coordinated by the AMA (Academy of Model Aeronautics) and the FCC (Federal Communications Commission). While there has been much debate and confusion over the changes, they're really fairly simple to understand and will ultimately make many more channels available for our use. Most of the radios in use today are compatible with the new frequency standards—at least, with the 40KHz spacing of the even-numbered channels—and they can be easily and inexpensively converted.

The "old" frequencies, which are no longer legal for use, and their designations were as follows:

Frequency	Flag Colors
72.080	Brown/White*
72.160	Blue/White
72.240	Red/White*
72.320	Purple/White
72.400	Orange/White
72.960	Yellow/White*
75.640	Green/White*

As you can see, this was only seven channels, and only the four marked by asterisks were reserved for aircraft use only, while the other three were shared with cars and boats. The old channels have been illegal for R/C use since December 20, 1987, and those frequencies are now being allocated to paging systems. Don't attempt to fight the sys-

tem by using the old frequencies; convert your radios to the new ones *now!* Since all channels in the 75MHz band are presently designated for surface use only (cars and boats), I won't discuss them further, other than to mention that, if you have an older radio on Green/White (75.640MHz), it can be converted to the new channels in the 72MHz band.

As of January 1, 1986, the following channels were phased in for aircraft use only:

Frequency	Channel #
72.030	12
72.550	38
72.590	40
72.630	42
72.670	44
72.710	46
72.750	48
72.790	50
72.830	52
72.870	54
72.910	56

A 7-channel exponential.

Between January 1, 1988, and January 1, 1991, the following aircraft-use-only channels have been added to the previous list:

Frequency	Channel #
72.070	14
72.110	16
72.150	18
72.190	20
72.230	22
72.270	24
72.310	26
72.350	28
72.390	30
72.430	32
72.470	34

Since January 1, 1988, channels 12 through 34 have been reserved for use by narrow-band transmitters (those capable of being used with a spacing of 20KHz between adjacent channels), while channels 38 through 56 may be used by either narrow-band transmitters or those not meeting narrow-band specifications. Note that, to provide an 80KHz buffer between channels 34 and 38, channel 36 isn't used. In practical terms, almost all older radios converted to the new frequencies can easily be used with a 40KHz spacing compatible with channels 38 through 56, while many, if not most, of those radios are proba-

Single-stick radio

bly capable of being used with a 20KHz spacing on your choice of any of the designated channels. In some cases, the receiver might not be capable of being successfully converted for use with a 20KHz spacing. In any case, have your transmitter checked/adjusted for frequency centering and bandwidth to be sure of their compatibility with the new standards.

Beginning January 1, 1991, the remaining frequencies between channel 11 (72.010) and channel 60 (72.990) will be filled in, giving us 50 channels in the 72MHz band reserved just for aircraft. The total frequency lineup in the 72MHz band will then be as follows:

Frequency	Channel #
72.010	11
72.030	12
72.050	13
72.070	14
72.090	15
72.110	16
72.130	17
72.150	18
72.170	19
72.190	20
72.210	21
72.230	22
72.250	23
72.270	24
72.290	25
72.310	26
72.330	27
72.350	28
72.370	29
72.390	30
72.410	31
72.430	32
72.450	33
72.470	34
72.490	35
72.510	36
72.530	37
72.550	38
72.570	39
72.590	40
72.610	41
72.630	42
72.650	43
72.670	44
72.690	45
72.710	46
72.730	47
72.750	48
72.770	49
72.790	50
72.810	51
72.830	52
72.850	53
72.870	54
72.890	55
72.910	56
72.930	57
72.950	58
72.970	59
72.990	60

While these frequencies have a uniform spacing of 20KHz, this doesn't necessarily mean that non-narrow-band radios will become obsolete on January 1, 1991. The AMA and FCC are constantly re-evaluating the frequency allocations in terms of actual use and practical implementation; it's quite probable that 40KHz spacing will be maintained between some channels in the upper range (channel 38 through 60) in order to allow the use of older radios. Still, if you're about to buy a new radio (or a used one, for that matter), you'd be wise to be sure it's of the narrow-band variety. Incidentally, no license is required for operators in the 72MHz band.

Once you've purchased your radio, or had an older one converted to one of the new frequencies, you'll need to be sure that its frequency is readily identifiable, both by yourself and the people with whom you fly. Getting "shot down" because some ignorant oaf turned on a radio on *your* channel takes a lot of the fun out of flying, to say the least, and the *last* person you want to be is the ignorant oaf who does the shooting! So please use the AMA standardized markings and check, *really check*, the frequencies of other fliers before turning on your radio. Figure 3-2 shows the AMA standard markings for a radio using channel 52 in the 72MHz band. According to the AMA, the wind streamer stating

"72MHz aircraft use only" should be approximately 1x8 inches and red. The color designates the band being used: red for 72MHz (aircraft use only), yellow for 75MHz (surface use only), and black for 50MHz (Amateur Radio Service only), about which, more will be presented shortly. Additionally, the channel number should be displayed on two white, vertically oriented plaques in $1^{1}/2$x$^{1}/4$-inch black numerals that are visible from both sides. These standardized wind streamers and channel-number plaques are readily available at local hobby and model stores.

Frequencies (27MHZ band)

Another band for which no operator's license is required is the 27MHz, or citizens band. The frequencies designated for radio-control use in this band are shared by both aircraft and surface users, and they're identified by single-color ribbons or flags. These frequencies and their associated colors are:

Frequency	Flag Color
26.995	Brown
27.045	Red
27.095	Orange
27.145	Yellow
27.195	Green
27.255	Green

Be aware that operation on these frequencies is subject to considerable interference from other users, and operation of model aircraft definitely *isn't* advisable.

Frequencies (50MHZ and 53MHZ bands)

These frequency bands (frequently referred to as 6-meter bands) are the exclusive province of amateur radio "hams" holding Technician, General, Advanced, or Extra Class licenses; holders of Novice licenses aren't authorized to use these bands.

In the 53MHz band, the following frequencies and their identifying ribbon colors are authorized:

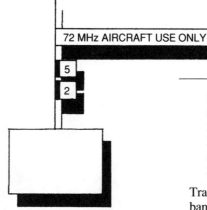

Fig. 3-2: Channel markings.

Frequency	Flag Colors
53.10	Black/Brown
53.20	Black/Red
53.30	Black/Orange
53.40	Black/Yellow
53.50	Black/Green
53.60	Black/Blue
53.70	Black/Purple
53.80	Black/Gray

Other Amateur Radio Service frequencies in the 6-meter band are identified by black and white, with the frequency inscribed on the white ribbon.

Frequencies in the 53MHz band are subject to interference from communication base and repeater stations on the 6-meter ARS (Amateur Radio Service) band, as well as when operating within approximately 10 miles of transmitters broadcasting on television Channel Two. For these reasons, R/C operation on the specifically designated and protected 50MHz-band channel is recommended only for holders of the appropriate ARS licenses.

As of January 1, 1988, the following frequencies in the 50MHz band have been allocated:

Frequency	Channel #
50.80	00
50.84	02
50.88	04
50.92	06
50.96	08

After January 1, 1991, five more channels will be added to these:

Frequency	Channel #
50.82	01
50.86	03
50.90	05
50.94	07
50.98	09

Transmitters operating in the 50MHz band should be marked with a black, 1x8-inch ribbon, and the channel numbers should be 1 inch wide and displayed on two vertically oriented $1^{1}/4$x$1^{1}/4$-inch square plaques

Other Frequencies

Holders of ARS licenses of General, Advanced, or Extra Classes may also use legal frequencies below 50MHz in the 6-meter band. Users of these frequencies should mark their transmitters with two wind streamers—one black and one white—and the frequency in use should be clearly indicated on the white (lower) streamer.

Frequency Interference

Much, probably too much, has been written about interference between certain R/C frequencies, especially in light of the new, closer spacing between frequencies. The primary types of interactive interference (we're ignoring radio interference sources outside the R/C bands here) to which our receivers are subject are:
- adjacent-channel interference
- second-order intermodulation (2IM)
- third-order intermodulation (3IM)
- image-frequency interference.

In practical terms, adjacent-channel interference can be eliminated by using only narrow-band equipment, paying special attention to the receiver design (dual-conversion receivers are best) and making sure your receiver is properly tuned. Be aware that although you might be suitably equipped, your buddies on the flight line might not be.

As for the other forms of interference, it's more important to know that you could be affected by them than to be burdened with the technical details. Setting theory aside, you can avoid any nastiness by standing at least 20 feet from other operating transmitters, and avoid flying your glider within 20 feet of them.

If you want to know which 2IM interference might cause you problems, add or subtract 455KHz from your frequency; the result will give you a frequency that could cause interference. For image interference, add or subtract 910KHz. And for those who insist on knowing which 3IM (the most likely) interference might "hit" them, doubling the channel number (or frequency; it doesn't matter which) of a particular radio, then subtracting the channel number (or frequency) of another radio, will yield the channel (or frequency) of the "hittable" radio. If you *really* want to work out all the possibilities, use a computer and have lots of paper handy. But why bother? If you think there's interference between other radios and yours, conduct a ground test with all the radios working; you'll know immediately if there really is any interference, and you'll easily be able to determine how far apart you must stand to eliminate it. You can also simply walk away from any other nearby radios.

Going by my experience, it's highly unlikely that you'll ever be bothered by R/C frequency interference, but you should be aware of its possibility. If you fly in contests, even a remote possibility of such interference will be eliminated by the assignment of frequency groupings and the separation of flying positions.

Receiver Tuning

While only holders of FCC commercial licenses are authorized to tune transmitters, anyone can tune his own receiver, and he'll do a good job of it, too. While we can assume that transmitters and receivers packaged together by a reputable manufacturer

A 7-channel dual-rate radio.

are precisely tuned to each other when delivered, this isn't necessarily—or even usually—so, because additional receivers or crystals are allowed a tolerance of .0025 percent. Obviously, if the transmitter crystal is at one end of this range and the receiver crystal is at the other, we might have a problem. Those who design our receivers have cleverly provided for adjustment of the IF (intermediate frequency) transformers in the receiver to bring everything into conformity.

To tune your receiver, you must first locate the IF transformers, so open the receiver and peek inside. You're looking for three small, rectangular, metal cans (probably in a row) with little screws in the top of each one, color-coded yellow, white, or black. If you can't find these cans, you probably have a dual-conversion receiver; button it back up and send it to a pro for tuning.

Assuming you've found the IF transformers, note the size of the slot in the head of each screw; you'll need a non-metallic screwdriver to fit that slot. Called tuning wands, these are readily available at electronics supply stores, or you can make one out of plastic, hardwood, or whatever. Now connect the receiver to your battery, servos and glider, grab your transmit-

ter and a buddy, and head for a large, open area.

On arrival, hand your transmitter (with its antenna collapsed) to your buddy, turn on both transmitter and receiver, and have your buddy walk away until control is lost, then walk toward you just until control is re-established. Using your tuning wand, turn the yellow-coded transformer screw clockwise until control is lost, and mark that position; then turn it counterclockwise until control is lost, and mark that position. Now turn the screw so that it's positioned midway between the two marks. Repeat this process with the white and black screws, in that order. Again, have your buddy walk away from you and position himself just at the limit of control; unless the receiver was perfectly tuned to begin with, he'll be farther away. Repeat the process, tuning (in order) the yellow, white and black screws, until you've achieved maximum range. Finally, after placing a drop of fingernail polish or wax on each screw to prevent it from turning, button up the radio, thank your buddy, and go fly!

Radio Care

The most important procedure in radio maintenance is proper charging of its Ni-Cd batteries. Ni-Cds have a memory; if you consistently fly for about half an hour and then recharge the batteries, the batteries will eventually only be able to put out one half-hour of energy. To avoid this, you should recharge the batteries only after they've been (almost) fully discharged. If you have a battery pack that has lost its full capacity, it can be restored by discharging it fully and then recharging it, and then repeating the cycle two or three times.

The easiest way to do this is by using an R/C System Analyzer-Rapid Charger, which is available from Astro Flight. This unit allows you to safely discharge your batteries, test their condition and recharge them rapidly at the field from your auto battery. If you're at home, use the System Analyzer to *discharge* the batteries and the trickle-charger that came with your radio to *recharge* them; rapid charging should be regarded as a field expedient and not as a normal procedure. Also, store your radio with the batteries fully charged, and recharge them every six months or so, even if they haven't been used.

As well as performing proper battery maintenance, you must protect your radio from excessive heat, vibration, liquids and dust. That's all that's required to ensure many years of trouble-free performance!

Building Tools and Techniques

CHAPTER 4

This chapter isn't intended to teach you how to build any particular model, but rather how to build models in general, with particular emphasis on the tools and procedures that will ensure success with your first, and subsequent, models. Carefully adhering to sound building methods will almost guarantee that you build straight, strong gliders that fly well "right off the bench."

Safety

When building a glider, you'll be subject to many potential safety hazards: sharp tools; flying debris; noxious and toxic chemicals; dusty, paint-laden air; and excessive noise are just a few of them. However, by using common sense, concentration and caution, you can make it through the experience alive!

You'll need:
- either shatterproof goggles or a face shield
- a sanding mask
- a suitable respirator (if you intend to do any spray painting indoors)
- either earplugs or hearing protectors.

Now, all you have to do is use these whenever it's appropriate. One more thing: Always remove your tie before going anywhere near any power tool!

Building Your First Glider

You'll get the most enjoyment out of your first glider if you regard it as a disposable learning vehicle, rather than a proud display of your craftsmanship. This isn't to say that it should be built sloppily, rather that it should not be so pretty or elaborate that you can't relax while flying it or experiment with new procedures without worrying about the inevitable repairs that follow the equally inevitable mistakes.

Along these lines, be sure to read the section on basic multi-purpose gliders in Chapter 1, pick a model suited to your interests and ability, and build it *exactly* according to the manufacturer's instructions, using the recommended materials and techniques. Assuming you've chosen the recommended basic 2-meter polyhedral design with built-up wings, I also strongly recommend that you use a colored, transparent, heat-shrink plastic film, such as MonoKote, to cover your first glider. This covering will enable you to easily determine the extent of any damage that results from those inevitable crashes.

Tools

You don't have to have a complete workshop to build model gliders; in fact, it's amazing what can be accomplished with a minimal collection of well-chosen hand tools. Of course, specialized hand tools and power tools do make the work a lot easier, but those who have more muscle than money needn't feel disadvantaged. Throughout this section, I'll try to differentiate between tools that are truly necessary, and those that are just handy to have. Of paramount importance is always buying the best quality tools available; you'll be rewarded with many years of trouble-free service and fine craftsmanship!

● **Building Board**. By far the most important tool is a good, flat building board, and I emphasize *flat*. To fly well, your glider must be straight and free of warps, and it's impossible to build a straight glider on a crooked surface.

The board should be at least 72 inches long and 18 inches wide, although I prefer one that's longer and wider, so that I can build several parts of the glider at once. Probably the best, and least expensive, source for a building board that can also serve as a work table is your local lumber yard or hardware store; they usually carry a good supply of building boards cleverly disguised as wooden hollow-core or foam-filled doors. Select a very smooth, perfectly straight one (use a metal straightedge and your eyeballs) that's made of a wood soft enough to accept pins. Avoid doors with blemishes, knots, or uneven spots.

When you've obtained a straight building board, keep it that way by mounting it on *level* legs (also available at the yard or store), level sawhorses, or a sturdy, level table. Be sure to support it in such a way that it can't sag in the middle. Take time to get it right, and set it at an appropriate height, and you'll be well-rewarded for your efforts. While you're admiring your new building board, take a few minutes to hang a bright, even light over it, too.

● **Shaping Tools**. Next to a good building board, your most important tool is a good, long, sanding block. No other tool will allow you to sand wings and fuselages quite as flat and even as a sanding block that measures at least 12x2 inches. This can be cut out of $3/4$-inch plywood (avoid other types of wood, since they might warp), or it can be made of T-shaped aluminum. I prefer plywood, as my large hands find it more comfortable to grip; those with smaller hands might prefer the aluminum.

As well as the long sanding block, you'll need several smaller square and rectangular blocks, and a collection of various sizes of doweling rods, or (my preference) acrylic rods and tubing, which, unlike wood, won't warp. These round sanding

blocks are great for sanding fillets and contouring surfaces. Small rubber blocks, which can bend and follow even the most complex surface curvatures, are also very helpful.

With all these blocks, while you can simply wrap the sandpaper around them and go to work, you might find it easier to glue the sandpaper to the block, especially when using smaller blocks or round ones. Supertape, which is a thin layer of adhesive somewhat similar to double-sided tape and obtainable from most hobby shops, is excellent for this. Gluing the sandpaper to the blocks saves both sandpaper and hands; give it a try.

Other useful shaping tools are a wood rasp, a small plane, a set of small jewelers' files, and, if you're feeling flush, a Dremel Moto-Tool kit will help make short work of an amazing number of otherwise tedious tasks.

● **Cutting Tools.** By far the most often-used cutting tool is a craft knife, such as a No. 1 X-Acto, equipped with a No. 11 blade. Be sure to get lots of those No. 11 blades; you'll go through them fast! You should also have a No. 2 knife with No. 2 blades, and a No. 5 knife with No. 19 blades. Other blades that are especially useful are the No. 16, No. 23, and No. 26. X-Acto also makes gouges, router and razor-saw blades that fit the handles listed above; all these cutting tools are much less expensive when purchased in boxed sets. You'll also appreciate having a Stanley knife and some single-edge razor blades in your shop. A 36-inch steel straightedge is an absolute must to complement your knife; using it is the only way to guarantee that you'll cut a straight line.

A razor saw is also necessary, and a miter box is a useful accessory to go with it. The miter box will ensure that your saw cuts are perfectly square, and it will also allow you to make cuts at precise angles. You'll also need a scrolling saw, or a small coping saw for cutting complicated shapes out of wood or metal sheeting, a pair of diagonal wire cutters and, perhaps, a pair of tin snips.

If your budget allows it, the Dremel Moto-Shop is a fantastic workshop aid that combines many useful functions. While it's basically a power jig and scrolling saw, on the side, it also has a power takeoff that can accept either sanding discs or a flex-cable-driven hand piece that can utilize all the Moto-Tool accessories.

At first, you probably won't need drills, but when you do, I recommend that you buy an electric one rather than a hand drill, as an electric drill allows you to hold the work piece in place with one hand while drilling with the other. Of course, a drill press is the best tool to ensure precise alignment while drilling; Dremel offers a good one for use with its Moto-Tool. When buying drill bits, be sure to get high-speed bits, as they last much longer and can drill much harder materials than wood bits. Purchase a small center punch along with your drill; it will mark the spot you want to drill, and it will prevent the drill bit from wandering as it enters the material.

● **Measuring Tools.** Two indispensable measuring tools are a metal yardstick and a 12-inch machinists' square (the type with an adjustable ruler that slides along, and can be clamped in a steel guide). The square is not only useful for measuring things, but it also serves as a 90-degree and a 45-degree marking and cutting guide. It can also be used to square-up tail surfaces, and it can even be used as a stripping guide for cutting balsa strips from sheets.

Other handy measuring tools include: a 12-inch metal ruler, a tape measure, a compass and pair of dividers, and a length of Dacron string (it doesn't stretch) for quickly dividing a given dimension into equal segments. Carbon paper and tracing paper make excellent tools for transferring dimensions from plans to parts.

● **Gripping Tools.** A vise is invaluable for holding things while you work on them. If you don't have room to mount a vise permanently on your work surface, there are versatile portable ones available. These can be clamped to any smooth surface by means of a lever-actuated suction cup.

As a minimum, you'll also need some regular pliers, a pair of slip-jaw mechanics' pliers and pair of long-nose pliers. You'll also appreciate having a pair of channel locks and a pair of vise-grips. Tape, C-clamps, clothespins and rubber bands are all useful for holding parts while you glue them together, or for establishing initial alignment before final assembly.

● **Fastening Tools**. The most basic fastening tool is a hammer, and you'll certainly need a small one. Lyman makes a perfect modeling hammer that has interchangeable steel, brass and plastic heads, and it's available in gun shops and sporting-goods stores. Also necessary are sets of slot-head and Phillips-head screwdrivers, jewelers' screwdrivers, and hexagonal Allen wrenches. You should also have a 6-inch crescent wrench, and you'll eventually want a set of small nut-drivers.

Something you probably won't need for your first glider, but are sure to need eventually, is a small soldering iron of about 40 watts, or so. Be sure to use only rosin-core solder, as

acid-core solder will corrode the parts on which it's used. For soldering piano wire only, use Sta-Brite silver solder.

Last, but certainly not least, keep a huge supply of T-pins for fastening parts to the plans and building bench while you're assembling them.

● **Finishing Tools**. If you're going to paint your model (and you will, if it's made of plastic or fiberglass) you'll need the usual brushes, rags, mixing cups, etc., that usually go along with any kind of painting job. Most wooden models are now covered with lightweight heat-shrink plastic film, such as MonoKote or Coverite. To apply these coverings, all you really need is a standard household iron, but the job will go much faster and more easily (and will look better, too) if you have a special MonoKote iron and a heat gun. The heat gun is especially useful for tightening covering that has slackened over time, for warping proper washout into wings, and for straightening warps.

● **Adhesives**. In the past, the most tedious thing about building a model was waiting for the glue to dry so that you could continue building and then waiting for it to dry again. With the advent of cyanoacrylates (CA) and epoxy, those days are over for good! Not only are the modern materials fast-setting and easy to apply, but, when properly applied, they're also much lighter and stronger than the older glues. Now, it's quite possible to build a glider using only CA and epoxy adhesives, and that's exactly what I recommend you do! One caution, though: Always, I repeat, *always*, wear eye protection when working with CA, because one tiny drop can easily cement your eyelids together—or worse!

Cyanoacrylates: Modern CAs, e.g., Zap, Jet and Hot Stuff, are truly a boon to modelers. Parts can be per-

manently joined in one or two seconds; an entire 6-foot built-up wing can be completely assembled in an evening; and the weight of the adhesive is negligible!

There's a variety of available CAs, each one best-suited to a specific task. The fastest, which sets in a second or two, is best for tight-fitting joints in porous woods. Be aware that it can, and will, if allowed, glue your fingers together just as well as it glues wood! For joints that aren't quite perfect, and for less porous hardwoods, most manufacturers offer a slow-setting CA with a higher viscosity that works perfectly.

Another type, which is very syrupy, is designed for filling gaps and will join many non-porous substances; it will even join surfaces that are oily or fuel-soaked! The last two types set in about a minute.

There's also a CA that takes about 20 seconds to set and is specifically intended for plastics. If any of these adhesives fail to set, or take longer than you want, a "kicker" (accelerator) is available, and this will cause them to set immediately.

A debonder is handy to keep around whenever you use any of the CAs. It's primarily intended for uncementing or cleaning stuck or coated fingers and cleaning drips of CA off work surfaces.

Epoxy: Generally, the faster an epoxy cures, the harder and more brittle it will be. Conversely, a slow-curing epoxy will be more flexible. Of primary interest to modelers are the 5-minute and 30-minute epoxies.

The 5-minute epoxy is best regarded as expedient for making field repairs, or when you want an extremely hard surface on a stationary part. The 15-minute epoxies are excellent for bonding wing center sections and for laminating reinforcing fiberglass cloth around them, and most modelers relegate 30-minute epoxy to laminating wooden wing skins to foam cores. Whichever you use, use as little as possible, as epoxy is heavy!

WARNING! Don't confuse epoxy adhesives with polyester resins, which use methyl-ethyl-ketone peroxide as a catalyst. MEKP is dangerous, as it's highly toxic, can cause severe burns, and can permanently turn your eye into a rock if it comes in contact with it. Primarily used by boat manufacturers for fiberglass-laminate lay-up, polyester resins must be used very carefully. They're excellent for laminating or finishing, but new, epoxy-based materials have been formulated to perform similar functions equally as well, and they are safer. Try to use only epoxy if the choice is available.

Getting Started

Whenever you start building a model, the first things you take out of the box should be the plans and the instructions. Study both until you have a clear understanding of how, and in what order, the model's parts should be assembled. You should follow the manufacturer's plans, instructions and building sequence *exactly*, until you're sufficiently knowledgeable (i.e., have enough building and flying experience) to modify a design. Actually, that's pretty good advice for everyone, regardless of their experience; I've seen a lot of gliders whose flight characteristics have been ruined by modelers trying to "improve" on the original design!

When you have a thorough understanding of the instructions, you should make an inventory of all the parts in the box. Become familiar with all the parts of the model, measuring each piece as you take it out of the box and comparing it with those shown on the plans. When you've identified all the parts and confirmed that they're all there, lay them out, grouped according to the sub-assembly in which they'll be used.

Now pin the plans to your building board and cover them with wax paper or clear plastic wrap; this will prevent your gluing the parts to the plans and will facilitate the cleaning up of potentially balsa-gouging drips of cured adhesive.

Construction

Apart from in one area, you'll achieve the lightest possible glider by using thin, fast-setting CA throughout construction. For the wing center section and other high-stress areas, epoxy is the best choice, and the instructions will tell you where to use it. When using CA, take care to fit each part closely and evenly to maintain an optimum bond. If you find yourself with a part that won't fit just right, e.g., a slightly short wing rib, either shim it with scrap material or use a gap-filling CA.

Almost all models are constructed in sub-assemblies that are subsequently joined to make the complete model. When building these, keep in mind that the completed model must balance laterally, i.e., from side to side. To ensure this, you'll have to use a scale, or construct a simple balance, to weigh the groups of parts for each sub-assembly, and then distribute the parts so that the right and left sides of each sub-assembly are equal in weight.

● **Fuselage.** When building the fuselage, it's absolutely critical that the right and left sides be of equal length and curvature with no warping. Additionally, the mounting surfaces for the wing and horizontal stabilizer must be even and at the proper angles of incidence. If the fuselage isn't perfectly straight and square, your glider will never fly well, so take special care to align all parts and surfaces when assembling it.

● **Wing.** Again, it's most important that the right and left sides of the wing be equal in weight. Be sure to pre-balance all the wing parts, and check the wing for overall balance once it's complete. If the completed wing is out of balance, correct it by adding a small amount of lead to the light wing tip.

For working on a built-up wing, you should make a simple tool that will help you align the wing ribs at a perfect 90-degree angle to your work surface, to which the leading and trailing edges should be pinned. Just take a piece of scrap wood or metal with a straightedge, and cut a notch in it that's equal to the thickness of each rib, and at a 90-degree angle to the straightedge. Slip this device over each rib to hold it perpendicular to the building surface while you're gluing it into place.

If you're building a sheeted foam wing, I've found Supertape ideal for laminating the sheeting to the foam core. Supertape is really just a film of adhesive with a paper backing. It's applied to the wing with its backing attached and rubbed hard to press it into the foam and heat it. Then you peel off the backing, press the wing skin onto the foam core (while the foam core is kept aligned in its cradle), sandwich the wing in both foam cradles, and keep weights stacked on the whole assembly overnight. It's light, strong, flexible, easy, and clean to handle; try it!

Whatever type of wing construction you're working with, take care to build it straight and warp-free. Steam-straighten, or replace, any warped wooden parts before building them into the wing.

● **Empennage.** Again, make sure that the tail feathers are straight and true while you're building them. Take special care to ensure that surfaces to be joined by hinges are perfectly straight; a close hinge gap is essential to the prevention of flutter (it can tear your glider apart), and it will improve its control response. This applies equally to ailerons, of course.

● **Final Alignment.** To stabilize the glider in flight (Fig. 4-1), the wing must have positive incidence (leading edge up) and the horizontal stabilizer, negative incidence (leading edge down), and there's a delicate balance between the two. Before attaching the empennage to the fuselage, re-check the fuselage to make sure the angle of incidence for the horizontal tail is as shown on the plans, and shim or sand it until it is. Do the same for the wing incidence angle.

through when the covering has been applied, so do a thorough job of sanding before you cover. If you're using the heat-shrink materials as recommended, don't use any dope or fillers on your glider, as they will blister and bubble when heat is applied in the covering process. Your

not a good choice for novice ground-bound R/C glider pilots; white gliders can *disappear* in the blink of an eye!

If you're using a household iron to cover your glider, set it between "cotton" and "wool"; if you have a MonoKote iron, turn it up all the way. Putting a single thickness of cotton

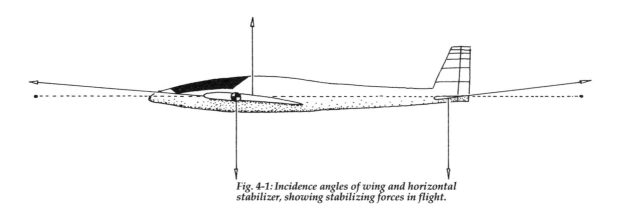

Fig. 4-1: Incidence angles of wing and horizontal stabilizer, showing stabilizing forces in flight.

When gluing-on the horizontal stabilizer, make sure it's at a perfect 90-degree angle to the fuselage center line and its lateral axis. You can do this by measuring from the nose to the tips of the horizontal stabilizer, and from the tips to the bench—assuming the fuselage is resting upright on it (Fig. 4-2). The vertical fin should be glued in place on, and precisely in line with, the fuselage center line, and at a 90-degree angle to the horizontal stabilizer. This, naturally, applies to conventional configuration gliders.

When installing the wing, make sure that the distances between each wing tip and the tail are equal, and that the wing is square with the fuselage. If the wing is removable and sits in wing beds, make sure that any rubber or foam used to keep it from shifting doesn't change the design incidence angle, or the wing's angle with the fuselage pitch axis.

Covering

Any blemishes or irregularities in the surfaces of your glider will show

final sanding should be with No. 400-grit sandpaper. When you're happy with your glider's finish, vacuum it thoroughly before starting the covering process.

I highly recommend Super MonoKote for covering your glider. It's light, waterproof, comes in a wide selection of both opaque and transparent colors, is easy to apply and maintain, and its rigidity will add a great deal of strength to your model. Besides, it comes with excellent covering instructions as part of the package!

I like to cover the top and bottom of my glider's wings and horizontal stabilizer in different colors, or to put a distinctive pattern on the top of the wing, to more easily follow (or identify, when I goof up!) the aircraft's attitude when it's performing aerobatics. Another good tactic, especially when you're first learning, is to cover one wing tip in a distinguishing color, thus allowing quick recognition of the glider's heading and attitude. By the way, while white is traditional for gliders and is demonstrably cooler for a pilot in the cockpit, it's usually

cloth over the iron yields a smoother finish, especially over large areas of sheeting or solid wood. Incidentally, if you're covering a sheeted foam wing, keep that iron moving and don't hold it in one place for too long; it can *melt* the foam underneath the sheeting. Another tip: Immediately before covering your glider, go over it thoroughly with an iron or, preferably, a heat gun. This will dry out the wood and prevent steam from forming bubbles under the MonoKote. Cover the top of the wings first, and then do the bottom. This will expedite repair, or replacement, of the covering where it's most likely to be damaged.

After covering a built-up wing, you'll undoubtedly find that the covering has shrunk unevenly and warped it. No sweat! Just get out your iron or heat gun, and twist the wing in the desired direction while applying heat to the covering. Continue until the wing is straight again. When the wing is straight, you'll have to use the same method to twist some washout into the wing tips. Twist the trailing edge of each wing tip upward according to the designer's instructions—usually about ¹/₄ inch or so—making sure both tips are equal (Fig. 4-3). Washout helps to stabilize your glider and prevent tip-stalling. (There's more on this subject in the next chapter.)

Radio Installation

The key points to watch for are that all controls move freely in the correct directions, and that the radio equipment is located optimally with regard to the glider's center of gravity.

After installing the hinges (no gaps, remember), check that all control surfaces are capable of full travel and move freely. Then, place all the radio equipment (including the unadjusted pushrods) in the fuselage where you think they ought to go, and assemble the glider. Attempt to balance the glider at the CG shown on the plans; a jig made of two eraser-tipped pencils set in a wooden block works well for this. Shift the radio equipment around, adding lead weights, if necessary, until the glider balances slightly nose-down at its design CG.

Once you've established where the radio equipment should go, mount it securely in place. If you pack the receiver in foam (you should), wedge or mount it so that there's no possibility of its shifting, then lead the antenna out through the fuselage and straight toward the rudder, stretching out the antenna to its full length. Make the wire ends connecting the control clevises to the pushrods as short as possible; excessive length here will result in "spongy" controls and can lead to control surface flutter.

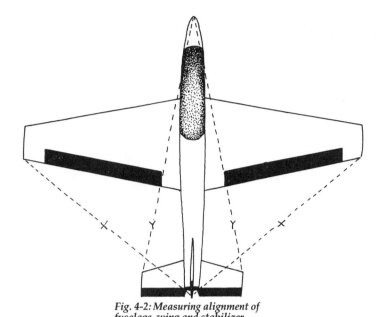

Fig. 4-2: Measuring alignment of fuselage, wing and stabilizer.

Finally, check all the controls for correct direction of travel. This sounds ridiculously obvious, but you'd be amazed how many fliers appear at the slope or field with control functions reversed (c'mon, I'm talking about their gliders!) Standing behind the glider, pushing the stick to the right should make the right aileron go up and the left aileron go down; if you only have rudder control, the rudder should move to the right. Pressing the stick forward should result in a downward deflection of the elevator; pulling it back should deflect it upward. If this isn't the case, flip reversing switches, change servos, or move pushrods, until they do.

While you're making the above tests, listen for servo "chatter." If

you hear it, you have a problem with a sticking control surface, a dragging pushrod, improper control-horn attachment, or all the above. Correct it *before* you fly, as such problems can drain your receiver battery and cause a crash! Also, make sure the control throws are adjusted to the designer's recommendations and that they're equal in both directions.

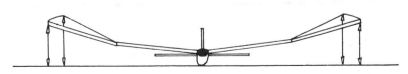

Fig. 4-3: Measuring wing washout.

Set-up, Trim and Adjustment

CHAPTER 5

Once your model is complete and the radio is installed, the next step is to ensure that it's in optimum flying condition. It's very common to see novice modelers come out to the flying site with gliders that are grossly out of trim, with warped control and flying surfaces, or even with controls installed backwards! To get the best performance from an aircraft, it must be built straight (and fixed, if it isn't straight), trimmed initially according to the manufacturer's specifications, and adjusted for proper control inputs and movements. Following the procedures outlined in this chapter will ensure a well-rigged glider that will fly well the first time you take it to the field or slope.

Since your glider's condition is subject to changes caused by temperature, humidity, accidents, etc., each time you go flying, you should run through these initial checks:

Check Fuselage for Warps

If your fuselage is warped, it's really a building problem rather than a set-up problem. Obviously, it's best to build a straight airplane to begin with, but some problems might not be fully evident until the glider is complete, or nearly complete. There are two fuselage warping problems that should concern you: lateral warping and twisting.

Lateral warping can be detected by sighting down the fuselage lengthwise. If the fuselage bends toward one side, then you have a real problem. A glider with a laterally warped fuselage will never fly straight, since one side of the fuselage will possess more drag than the other and air will not flow equally around it. The best, and perhaps only, solution to this is to cut the fuselage apart and rebuild it. If the fuselage is wooden and not yet covered, you can try to correct the warp by holding the fuselage over steam and applying pressure to correct the fault. Be aware that this remedy might be only temporary, as the warping stresses in the wood may manifest themselves again when humidity changes. With wood, I recommend cutting it apart to relieve the stresses and then gluing it together again while aligned properly. If the fuselage is made of plastic or fiberglass, it can be straightened by applying heat with a heat gun or boiling water, and bending the fuselage into alignment, holding it in position until it cools.

To check for a twisted fuselage, sight down the length of the fuselage from the tail. The vertical stabilizer should be aligned perfectly with the vertical center line of the fuselage, while the horizontal stabilizer should be at a perfect right angle to that. If this isn't the case, the problem can often be corrected by cutting the tail surfaces free of the fuselage, reshaping the fuselage mounting surface to make it square, and then remounting the vertical and horizontal tail surfaces in proper alignment. Another, although less desirable, option is to ignore the fuselage misalignment and alter the wing mounting, either by shimming at the wing butts or by bending the wing rods to align with the tail. While the glider will fly fairly well, it will certainly look a little weird in flight.

Obviously, the best solution to warping problems is to build straight to begin with, but then, I'm assuming you're checking out someone else's glider!

Check Wing for Warps

Assuming you're dealing with a built-up Mylar-covered wing, rather

Fig. 5-1: Measuring wing washout.

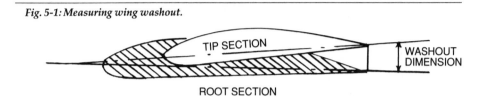

than sheeted foam, which can't be straightened if warped, check the center wing sections on both sides of the center dihedral joints for warps by holding down each section of the wing on a flat surface, e.g., a building board. If the wing has a flat-bottomed or under-cambered airfoil, both the leading and trailing edges should make uniform contact with the board. If the wing has a symmetrical or semi-symmetrical airfoil, weight or pin the wing so that the trailing edge is flush with the surface of the board, then measure the height of the leading edge at several points to ascertain that the wing is straight and flat. If it isn't, the wing can easily be straightened by applying localized heat to the Mylar covering with either an iron or a heat gun, while simultaneously twisting the wing slightly beyond the amount of correction desired. When it has cooled, check the wing again and continue the process as often as necessary until the wing is straight.

Check and Adjust Washout

Washout is the slight bending of the wingtips so that the trailing edge is higher than the leading edge at the tip (Fig. 5-1). In flight, this effectively reduces the tip's angle of attack in relation to the rest of the wing, thus reducing tip-stalling tendencies and increasing the stability of the glider. It's important that the washout be set according to the manufacturer's specifications, as too little will result

in tip-stalling, while too much will create excess drag and a "wallowing" tendency. It's also quite common to find gliders at the flying site with more washout on one wingtip than on the other, and this results in a glider that wants to turn *all* the time.

To adjust and/or correct washout, weight or pin the wing center section to the building board and measure the height of the leading and trailing edges at the tips. The trailing edge should be about $1/4$ to $3/8$ inch higher than the leading edge at that point, or whatever the manufacturer or designer has specified on the plans. If this isn't the case, use an iron or heat gun to heat the Mylar covering, while simultaneously twisting the wing's tip section in the desired direction. Let the covering cool and measure again, continuing the process until the washout is correct. When you're satisfied with the results on one side, repeat the process on the other, making sure the washout on both wing panels is identical.

Check Decalage

Decalage is a French word referring to the wing's angle of incidence. The wing incidence angle is measured relative to a line passing from nose to tail on the center line of the airplane. The wing will have a positive angle (leading edge up) relative to this line, while the horizontal stabilizer will have a negative angle (leading edge down). This is because, to maintain

stable flight, the resulting downward pressure on the horizontal stabilizer must balance the lifting pressure created by the glider's movement through the air (Fig. 5-2). Make sure these incidence angles are set according to the plans. They can be adjusted either by sanding or shimming the mounting surfaces.

Within limits, a glider featuring a full-flying horizontal stabilizer, or stabilator, isn't sensitive to wing incidence angle, since the stabilator can correct for any discrepancy. Still, it's best to set the decalage according to the designer's plans.

Balance Wings

While you undoubtedly weighed and balanced the wood, or other materials, for each wing while building (you did do that, didn't you?), the spanwise balance should be checked again, and corrected if necessary, after the glider has been covered and the radio installed. This check should be made with the glider fully assembled and in a ready-to-fly configuration. It's necessary to test and balance the entire glider, instead of just the wing, because some imbalance might have been introduced, owing to an asymmetrical radio installation in the fuselage, as well as to unequal hardware installation, adhesive application, covering, or painting.

With the glider fully assembled, support it with pins pressed into the center of the nose and tail at a location at, or slightly above, the glider's horizontal center line (pitch axis). The backs of two chairs make a good support for the pins while you check and adjust the balance. With the glider thus supported, any spanwise imbalance will be readily apparent,

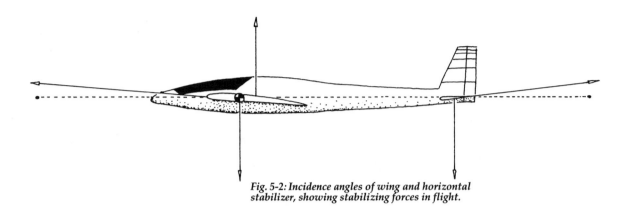

Fig. 5-2: Incidence angles of wing and horizontal stabilizer, showing stabilizing forces in flight.

as the glider's heavy wing will tend to roll downward.

If the glider remains level, congratulate yourself on your superior building ability and extraordinary good fortune, move on to the next sections, then go fly. The rest of us will need to add weight to the light wing in order to properly balance the glider. This is easily done by placing a small piece of lead that's slightly heavier than necessary at the tip of the light wing, then trimming the lead until the wing just balances. Carefully cut a pocket in the bottom of the wing to fit the lead weight, glue it into place, then cover or paint over it.

Check Center of Gravity

At least for the initial flights, the center of gravity (CG) should be located where shown on the plans. If you have no plans, or if it isn't shown on them, start with the CG located one-third of the wing chord behind the leading edge, measured at the wing/fuselage junction.

This adjustment is best made with a simple tool made of a wooden block and two ordinary pencils (the kind with an eraser attached). To make one, lay a block of wood flat on the bench to serve as a base, then drill two suitable holes for the pencils in it, spacing them so that they'll straddle the fuselage where the wings attach. Cut the pencils to a length that will

support the glider off the bench, then press and glue them into the holes.

To check and adjust the CG, lightly place a strip of masking tape chord-wise (from leading to trailing edge) on the bottom surface of each wing near the wing roots. Next, carefully locate the position of the CG as indicated on the plans, and mark this position on the masking tape. Now, place the glider on the pencil jig so that the CG marks on the masking tape rest atop the pencils' erasers. The glider should balance at this point, but without further adjustments, they rarely do.

If the glider doesn't balance at the CG, attempt to rearrange the radio equipment so that it will. Adding lead to correct an improper CG location should be regarded as a last resort, as the glider should ideally be as light as possible. If the glider is tail-heavy, make sure the battery is stuffed as far into the nose as possible. If that doesn't do it, try moving the servos and receiver forward to achieve the correct balance. If that *still* doesn't correct the situation, you'll have to add lead as far forward as possible— or aft, if the glider is nose-heavy (you should be so lucky!)—in any quantity that's necessary to make the glider balance at the CG. Once you've determined the proper amount and position of added ballast, make sure you fasten it securely so that it won't shift in flight!

Check Controls

At this point, I recommend that you disconnect all control rods from their servos and double-check the control surfaces and functions for complete freedom of movement. Many instances of control binding or inhibited movement don't manifest themselves until the glider is fully assembled. It's absolutely imperative that all control surfaces move freely throughout, and slightly beyond, their full range of travel. If you find anything amiss, do whatever is necessary to fix the problem before reconnecting the control rods to the servos. Care taken here will be well rewarded.

When you're sure that all controls function freely, reconnect the control rods and servos, then turn on the transmitter and receiver and check for correct direction of control movements. It's amazing how many planes arrive at the field or slope with control functions reversed. This is an easy error to make for those who use the same transmitter with different airplanes! The most common problem is with the ailerons, so make sure that when you move the stick to the right, the right aileron goes up and the left aileron goes down. Any problems in this area can be solved by substituting a servo that turns in the proper direction (servos come in both right and left orientations) and, if possible, relocating the control rod to the opposite side of the servo, or by simply flipping the servo-reversing switch, if you're fortunate enough to own one of the more modern and/or sophisticated radios that have this feature.

When we've ascertained that the controls are moving in the correct directions, we need to adjust them for the correct amount of movement. Admittedly, this adjustment will differ according to each individual's preference for more or less glider sensitivity to control inputs, but I again recommend that you adhere to the designer's specifications for the initial flights. If you don't have any specifications for your glider, $3/4$- to 1-inch total throws ($3/8$ to $1/2$ inch either side of neutral) on rudder and elevator, and $3/8$-inch to $1/2$-inch total throws on the ailerons should provide a reasonable starting point.

To set the control throws, first center all the transmitter trim sliders, then adjust the lengths of the control rods so that all control surfaces are in their neutral positions. The control throws are then adjusted by moving the control rods in or out on the servo arms and/or control horns until the proper travel is established. Make sure that control travel is the same in both directions for each control function, unless, of course, differential movement is desired. If you detect any undesired differential movement of the controls, check to be sure the coupling to each control horn is exactly over the hinge line, and that aileron torque rods and their control rods intersect at a 90-degree angle. If they don't, change them so that they do.

If you have a dual-rate radio, these throws should be adjusted with the radio set on high rate (maximum throw). If your radio features transmitter end-point adjusting, set the transmitter potentiometers to maximum while adjusting the control throws, and reserve the end-point adjustment feature for any necessary

post-flight or in-flight fine-tuning. Setting up your radio and control throws in this way will provide the greatest servo resolution.

Range-Check Radio

Range-checking is a very simple procedure that will ensure your radio system is working properly. It should be done before each day's flying.

To perform this check, first collapse or remove the transmitter's antenna (whichever the manufacturer recommends). With both the transmitter and receiver on, check the glider for proper control responses, while slowly walking away from it. You should be able to achieve a distance of 30 to 50 feet before the controls start to chatter, or lose their responsiveness. If this is the case, fly. If not, check the transmitter and receiver for amount of charge, loose connections, etc. If you can't isolate and correct the problem, the radio system should be returned to the manufacturer for repairs.

Test Glide

While an experienced pilot might be able just to throw an untried glider off a slope or hi-start and keep ahead of the problems, in the interests of aircraft longevity and personal peace of mind, I strongly recommend test-gliding every new glider over a flat, preferably soft, area. Not only does this procedure permit you to thoroughly check out the glider, but it also allows the glider to check out the pilot! Test-gliding is best done with an assistant, whose presence allows the pilot to concentrate fully on flying, and the following discussion assumes you have a helper.

After once again range-checking the radio system and the control throws, the assistant should hold the glider beneath its wing and run forward until the wing develops lift, but he/she shouldn't release the glider yet. If the glider doesn't seem to want to lift, slide the elevator trim pot in the up-elevator direction and try

again. Repeat this as often as necessary until the glider feels light in hand as your helper runs forward. Now have him/her run somewhat faster and, with the nose pointed at the horizon and the wings level, thrust (don't throw) the glider straight forward and release it. Now, watch it go.

If the glider flies straight forward and glides to a smooth landing about 50 feet away, all is well. Go fly and be grateful! If the glider noses steeply downward, the CG is too far forward and you'll have to lighten your glider by removing some weight from the nose. If it noses sharply upward and stalls, then the CG is too far aft, and the radio equipment will have to be moved forward, or weight will have to be added to the nose (Fig. 5-3). Be aware that stalling can also be caused by a flying speed that's much higher than the tested trim speed, and this is usually caused by an over-enthusiastic launch (Fig. 5-4). So keep your assistant under control and correct the problem with a little down trim.

If the glider tends to turn, correct this with aileron and/or rudder trim in the direction opposite the direction of the turn (left trim to correct for a right turn, and vice versa). Make these changes a little at a time, because massive changes can result in massive damage! Remember that your glider was *supposed* to be perfectly adjusted before it ever reached the test-gliding stage, so it shouldn't be too far off.

When you have the glider trimmed and the CG adjusted so that it glides smoothly and straight "hands off," note the control-surface positions, return the transmitter trim sliders to neutral, and use the pushrod/torque rod and clevis adjustments to return the control surfaces to their tested neutral positions. This is also a good time to adjust the control response (longer or shorter control throws) to your preference. Test-glide the aircraft once again to be sure it glides straight and smoothly with no control inputs and with the transmitter trims set at neutral. Once this has been achieved, you're ready to really cut loose and go flying—knowing, not guessing, exactly how your glider will behave! Well ... for the most part, anyhow!

glider, rather than a ground speed (the glider's speed across the ground). But since model gliders lack air-speed indicators, how in the world are we to accurately judge these air speeds? The answer is pitch attitude.

what faster than minimum sink speed, and it's best determined by experimentation. Start from minimum sink speed and gradually increase the down trim until the glider seems to climb "on the step" and

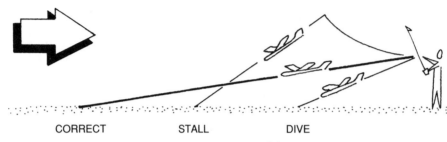

CORRECT   STALL   DIVE

Fig. 5-3: Test glide.

In-Flight Trimming for Performance and Conditions

Probably the main factor that sets the experienced glider pilot apart from those who are less experienced, both in competition and in sport flying, is the ability to trim the aircraft for maximum performance at all times. Simply put, the experienced pilot is always flying the glider at the edge of its capabilities, while the less experienced pilot is content to haul it around the sky any way that seems to work. Those who always seem to climb higher and faster, who get in one or two more aerobatic maneuvers, who get more duration and/or distance, and whose batteries even seem to last longer (they do!) even when they're flying the same glider as everyone else, have mastered one great skill: They know how to trim a glider for maximum flight performance in the prevailing conditions and soon, so will *you!*

To trim our glider to attain the maximum performance of which it's capable, we need to know three key speeds: minimum sink speed, maximum L/D speed and best penetration speed. It's important to note that each of these is an *air speed,* i.e., it's relative to the air mass surrounding the

The pitch attitude of the glider (the degree to which the nose is raised above or lowered below a neutral position relative to the horizon) is the best indicator of the wing's angle of attack, (its angle to the relative wind), and it's thus also the best indicator of the glider's air speed. Bearing this in mind, let's take a closer look at our three important air speeds.

● **Minimum Sink Speed:** Minimum sink speed gives the glider the maximum amount of time aloft from a given altitude. This speed is the one to use when circling in thermals for altitude or at all times when in need of the maximum lift that the glider can produce. To determine the glider's pitch attitude at this air speed, slow the glider until it just stalls, then trim it to fly (not mush) at a speed just above the stall break. Memorize this pitch attitude, and you'll be able to return at will to minimum sink speed without stalling.

● **Maximum Lift/drag (L/D) Speed:** Maximum L/D speed allows the glider to fly the greatest distance from a given altitude. Use this speed when traveling from one thermal to another, or at any time when you want to, or have to cover the maximum possible ground. This is a moderately fast, stable air speed, some-

really perform, or, if blessed with still air and enough room, actually measure the distance from a known altitude (ground effect will interfere with this, however). Maximum L/D speed is a good speed for a glider, and one at which you'll undoubtedly fly more often than any other, so take some time to play with it and learn it well.

● **Best Penetration Speed:** Best penetration speed permits the glider to travel forward against the wind and/or thermal as rapidly, and as far over the ground, as possible. This speed will vary with the conditions. It's primarily used for escaping from excessive lift (or sink), such as that produced by a strong thermal or wave, or for regaining position in front of or over a slope for a glider accidentally (I hope!) flown behind it and in danger of being caught in the rotor. It's also frequently used to regain control of an inadequately ballasted glider being blasted about by very strong winds (more about that later). It's a very fast speed with a pronounced nose-down attitude—an attitude that doesn't remain constant, because it varies according to the direction and strength of the wind and/or lift components. You'll be able to recognize the results! Simply fly the glider to cover the most ground as rapidly as possible.

At this point, I must emphasize that these are trim speeds. To extract the maximum performance from your glider, you must use the trim potentiometer on your transmitter to set these speeds and maintain them. This is because no matter how smooth a pilot you might think you are, you can't hold the stick as still as the trim pot can. You'll inevitably induce small control movements through the stick, thus creating unnecessary drag, as well as increased battery drain. So, for maximum performance, use the trim pot! That's one of the primary facts that will help you to become an experienced pilot.

If you take the time to learn and practice these air speeds for your glider(s), always choosing and using the appropriate one for prevailing conditions, I guarantee a quantum leap in your flying ability. More information about the practical uses of these three important speeds can be found in the sections on thermal soaring and slope soaring.

needs or flying style, or for the prevailing conditions. Slight changes in CG location can make significant differences to a glider's handling characteristics.

For instance, moving the CG forward will generally make the glider more stable and resistant to abrupt changes in attitude. A forward CG shift can be used to increase overall stability, or it can be used to help a glider cope with gusty winds.

Conversely, moving the CG aft will tend to make a glider less stable and, therefore, more responsive to control inputs. Thus, a rearward shift in CG can be used to enhance a glider's aerobatic performance. Depending on a glider's design, a rearward CG shift might help to reduce the amount of elevator deflection that's necessary to properly download the tail section, so it results in better airflow around the horizontal stabilizer and, therefore, less drag. In light winds or calm conditions, this could mean the difference between achieving a duration goal or landing early.

It's important that any CG changes

gish, draggy, unresponsive glider that, when pushed to extremes, might not be able to recover from stalls and/or spins, or even be able to fly at all. Too much weight aft will result in a "squirrelly," ultrasensitive glider that might be so unstable that it's uncontrollable. Take it a little at a time; the difference in performance will be readily apparent, and your glider will tell you when you're about to go, or have gone, too far!

Take the time to experiment with your glider(s) and determine the CG range within which you can safely make changes. I like to make notes of my CG experiments, noting the conditions prevailing at the time and the glider's response, and I keep the notes in my flight kit so that I can refer to them at the flying site and make known, proven adjustments in my glider's flying characteristics. You'll be amazed at the difference even very slight changes can make!

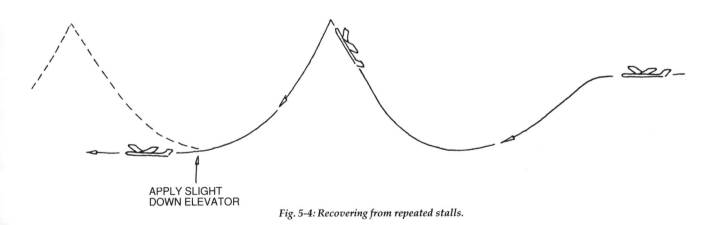

APPLY SLIGHT
DOWN ELEVATOR

Fig. 5-4: Recovering from repeated stalls.

Fine-Adjusting CG

While the CG shown on the plans is located where the designer feels optimum overall glider performance of the glider will result, it might not be optimally located for your particular

be made *very* gradually, about 1/4 inch at a time for conventional gliders, and 1/8 inch at a time for flying wing and canard designs. The goal here is to improve the glider's performance, not to destroy it altogether. Too much weight forward will result in a slug-

Ballasting

After having gone to great extremes to design (or buy) and build a glider that's as light as possible, it might seem counterproductive to add weight to "improve" its performance, but under certain conditions, that's *exactly* what we can do!

For instance, you might have flown your glider at a slope site on a day when the wind was blowing significantly more strongly than usual, and you discovered that not even best-penetration speed trim would allow your glider to penetrate upwind under those conditions. Or perhaps you've been thermal soaring in strong wave or convective conditions, and you found that, you spent all your energy and time just trying to keep your glider in sight, rather than practicing aerobatics or leisurely cruising as you'd planned. Or maybe you wanted to beat a friend in a pylon race, but your glider just wouldn't fly fast enough.

What can be done to change all this next time? Well, the alternatives are: stay home, build a new glider to fit those situations, or add ballast to the glider you have!

By adding ballast, the glider's wing loading will be increased. This will result in an increase of all the glider's trim speeds, as well as its stall speed (there's no free lunch!), and it will allow it to penetrate better and fly faster, while also increasing its stability in turbulence. Happily, while the trim air speeds are increased, we can still recognize, set and maintain them by their pitch attitude, which remains unchanged. On the down side, the structural loads on the glider are also increased, as is its sink rate relative to the surrounding air. In addition, because of the glider's increased stall speed, you'll be landing at a higher air speed and probably (depending on headwind) a proportionally higher ground speed. Pick your landing site carefully!

So how much ballast do we add and where do we put it? Add whatever it takes, but don't over-stress the airframe. We add it at, or around, the CG so that the resultant stress is distributed over those areas of the airframe best able to handle it.

In more specific and practical terms, there are two choices:

- Build hollow tubes in the wings into which weight can be added in the form of lead shot or lead rods
- Add weight in the form of lead "slippers" that fit into the fuselage and are centered about the CG.

Of course, we can combine both techniques if we need lots of ballast. Building ballast tubes into the wing is preferred, as it distributes the weight throughout the wing itself, thus reducing stresses at the wing roots where they join the fuselage.

When building ballast tubes into the wing, the maximum tubing diameter will be structurally obvious, but it's important that the tubing isn't longer than one-third of the span length of each wing panel. This will prevent stiffening the wing unduly and possibly introducing unbearable stress at the outboard end of the ballast tubing/wing panel juncture.

The usual method of filling the tubing (using No. 8 or No. 9 lead shot) is by drilling a hole into it through the bottom of the wing and sealing it with a custom-fit plug or piece of tape when the lead has been inserted. If the tubing is to be only partially filled with shot, be sure to fill the rest of the tubing with small plastic beads, beans, or some other filler material to keep the ballast from shifting during flight, and be sure to double-check the aircraft's spanwise balance before flying, or you could be in for a nasty surprise! If your glider's design is such that the wing separates, allowing access to the wing roots, you might prefer to leave the inboard end of the tubing open and to cast lead plugs of various weights to fit inside the tubing. These can be held in place by lengths of wooden doweling. The advantage of this method is that it's easier to add known amounts of ballast and, as long as the ballast plugs in each wing are equal in weight, the spanwise balance needn't be rechecked each time you load the tubing.

If you prefer to add ballast to the fuselage, you'll have to cast lead "slippers" that are shaped to fit a fuselage compartment, or compartments, centered at the glider's CG.

Make sure these are a snug fit so they can't shift during flight.

While this method of ballasting does create added stress at the wing/fuselage juncture, it does have the advantage of enabling you to add known weights, and it eliminates the need to recheck spanwise balance, although you'll have to recheck the fore/aft balance when first setting up this system.

Finally, before you drop (press?) one of those snug-fitting weights into the ballast compartment, think about how you'll get it back out! A length of flat ribbon running under the "slipper," or a screw driven into the top of it, are a couple of ways of solving this problem.

As for how much weight to add, start with 20 percent of the glider's total weight and work up from there. The maximum that can be stuffed into wing tubes will probably be about 50 percent of the glider's weight. Further weight will have to be added to the fuselage. And please, unless you like building a lot more than you like flying, be sure to thoroughly flight-check your glider's ability to carry this weight, on tow and in flight, before you load it with everything that can be stuffed into it and go for broke (pun intended!). While your tests will preferably be carried out in still air, remember that turbulent conditions will increase the stresses on your glider manifold. It pays to be conservative here!

If you've just read this chapter, or any part of it, for the first time, please take the time to go over all of it again thoroughly. If you follow the steps outlined, I guarantee that your glider will perform at its maximum design capability, and it will *outperform* any similar glider that hasn't been "tweaked" to the same degree. In addition, the sections on in-flight trimming, fine-adjusting CG, and ballasting will ensure that you'll be flying your glider in such a way that you extract the maximum from it under all conditions, and that adds up to a winning combination, for sure!

Thermal Soaring

The great advantage of thermal soaring is that it can be done in almost any place and at any time. All you need is a relatively flat site that's large enough to launch and land a glider and differential heating of the surrounding landscape. Thermal soaring provides the glider pilot with

Winch-launch at the Rose Bowl, Pasadena, CA, and an open-class glider.

a never-ending challenge in locating and utilizing invisible and elusive columns, bubbles and currents of warm, lifting air. Glider pilots also take pride in the considerable skill necessary to sustain flight for ex-

tended periods where a non-flier or novice wouldn't think it possible.

The sight of a glider or sailplane soaring gracefully against a backdrop of clouds and sky is truly magnificent, and as we learn the secrets of the hawks and eagles, the sky becomes our domain, too! If you want to measure your achievements against those of others, there's a wide offering of goal-oriented programs and contests from which to choose. Whatever your interest, thermal soaring offers challenges and rewards aplenty, but first, you have to get airborne!

Launching Methods

● **Hi-Start**. The hi-start, or bungee launch, (Fig. 6-1) is the most common method of glider launching in the United States. The hi-start has the advantages of being simple, inexpensive, effective and easily portable. A lone pilot equipped with a glider, a radio and a hi-start is well-prepared for enjoying his or her sport almost anywhere.

A hi-start is usually made of a length of surgical rubber tubing connected to a length of nylon line or monofilament, which in turn is connected to a swivel, a small parachute and a metal ring fastened to the top of the parachute (Fig. 6-2). The free end of the rubber tubing is attached to a stake driven into the ground at the upwind end of the launch area, while the ring at the parachute end is slipped over a hook affixed to the underside of the glider. The whole rig has been stretched to several times its original length. The glider is then released from the pilot's or a helper's hand and towed aloft to heights of several hundred feet by the energy stored by the surgical tubing. At the apex of the launch, the glider is flown off the tow ring, whereupon the parachute, which has been held closed by the line tension, will open and lower the hi-start to the ground in a downwind direction where it can be retrieved and stretched out for another launch.

Obviously, the strength of the surgical rubber tubing should be matched to the size of the glider. The best way to be assured of this is to purchase the ready-made or kitted hi-starts available from several different manufacturers and classified according to the weight and size range of the

A good rule of thumb for properly stretching a hi-start assembled from these materials, or one similar to it, is to use one long pace for each inch of your glider's wingspan. Should you decide to use stronger surgical tubing than that I've listed, be sure to increase the strength of the other components as well. Also, do yourself and everyone else nearby a favor, and use a screw-in type of anchor instead of a

it easier to set up on the field the next time I go flying. Finally, store it in a cool, dark place.

For tips on tow-hook placement, glider setup and hi-start launching techniques, read the section entitled "Hi-Start and Winch-Launching Technique" immediately following the winch-launching section.

● **Winch Launch**. For obvious reasons of cost, complexity and weight, most electric winches are club projects and used primarily for club-sponsored contests, practice sessions and fun-flys (another very good reason for joining a club). Once set up, they're extremely convenient and easy to use, especially if equipped with an electric line retriever (Fig. 6-3). A tremendous number of launches can be achieved in a minimum time using a winch and retriever and, skillfully operated, they can launch just about anything that can be made to fly.

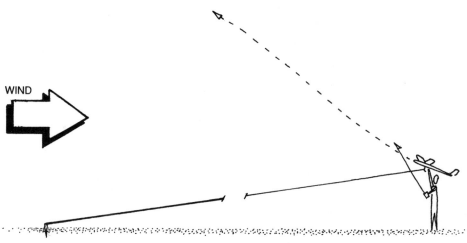

Fig. 6-1: Launching with a hi-start.

WIND

STAKE   SURGICAL TUBING   NYLON LINE

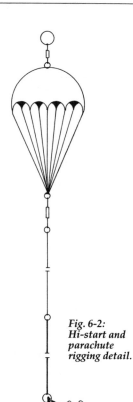

Fig. 6-2: Hi-start and parachute rigging detail.

gliders for which they are suitable. These generally cost less than the retail price of the components purchased separately, and most come complete with a reel and stakes. If you insist on making your own, here's a list of components for a hi-start that's suitable for gliders of the 72- to 100-inch categories:
- 100 feet of surgical rubber tubing; $^3/_{16}$-inch i.d., $^1/_{16}$-inch wall thickness
- 400 feet of 40-pound test-nylon monofilament, or 450 feet of 45-pound test-nylon squidding line
- two swivels, 50-pound test
- two steel or brass rings
- parachute with shroud lines continuing to center of canopy
- two steel tent stakes with wide collars, at least 12 inches long or, preferably, at least one spiral stake
- a reel to hold the assembled hi-start

straight tent stake. These are usually available at pet stores. At the other end of the scale, for those with 2-meter or light, standard-class gliders and limited space, an alternative to a full-size hi-start is the Craft-Air Up-start, which permits launches of about 200 feet from any 300-foot field.

Try not to step on your hi-start, but if it does break or get nicked, the rubber can be repaired by inserting a length of wooden doweling into the two halves. Wash off any chemicals with which the rubber tubing might have come in contact, then dry it thoroughly. Before storing it, dust the rubber with *pure* talcum powder. Don't use baby powder, or anything that contains perfumes, as the chemicals will attack the rubber. I like to roll my hi-start on the reel with the rubber part last; this makes

If you want to build a winch, there are many sources of specific plans, but you'll probably be better off understanding the general principles and utilizing whatever materials you find locally. The photographs and illustrations accompanying this section depict winches and retrievers designed and built by Toni Stark for the Pasadena Soaring Society of Pasadena, CA. While they reflect an unusually high degree of engineering and craftsmanship, the principles involved are common to all such devices.

Referring to the diagram of a complete winch and retriever setup (Fig. 6-4), the most commonly used motors (No. 4) are Ford long-shaft (5 3/4 inch) 12V automotive starter motors powered by either 6V or 12V batteries. Hubs for these are available from Dynaflite Models, and they're available with a 4-inch hub diameter for use with a 6V battery, or a 2-inch hub diameter for use with a 12V battery. The 6V-powered winch provides a soft, easily controlled launch, while the 12V version has considerably more power and requires more skill in operation. The speed of the winch is regulated by rapidly pulsing the foot switch (No. 6) and, yes, it's possible to snap a glider's wings with the force available, so go easy when first learning to use a winch! On the winch's electrical diagram, note that the foot switch activates a solenoid, which in turn connects the battery to the starter motor. Solenoids have been known to fail, and this results in a potentially dangerous runaway winch, so, when building your winch, be sure to include a large, easily reached emergency knife-switch (Fig. 6-5)!

A brake (No. 3) of some sort, actuated by a lack of line tension, is needed to prevent overruns when launching and backlashes when using a retriever. The most commonly used brakes are bicycle coaster brakes or motorcycle brakes. A line guide is

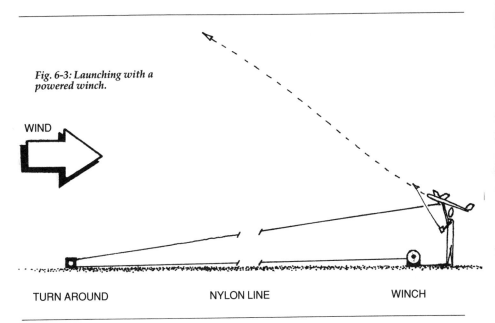

Fig. 6-3: Launching with a powered winch.

WIND

TURN AROUND   NYLON LINE   WINCH

attached to the actuating arm of the brake in such a manner that the winch drum will be free to turn as long as the line is under tension, but will be slowed whenever the tension is released.

In spooling the line (No. 2) on the drum, use 120-pound test nylon cord, and be aware that current FAI rules specify that the maximum distance allowed from which to turn around is 200 meters, with a maximum line length of 400 meters (1,312.33 feet). Incidentally, a bicycle hub mounted between brackets fastened to a plate that can be staked firmly to the ground, works well for a turnaround (No. 1). If you aren't using a line retriever, a swivel, parachute (No. 9), second swivel and tow-hook ring (No. 8) rigged as with a hi-start, complete the line setup.

An electric retriever will expedite use of the winch and eliminate the work involved in having to chase down the end of the line after each launch. The retriever works in much the same way as an open bail spinning reel. A length of 45-pound test-nylon squidding line (No. 7) leads from the rim of the large-diameter reel (12 to 18 inches or so) on the retriever, through a large circular

guide (12) placed several feet in front of the reel, and is fastened to the heavy tow line at a point below the parachute. As the winch pulls the glider aloft, the retriever line follows, free-spooling over the rim of the retriever spool. As soon as the glider is released, the retriever operator hooks the retriever line around a hook (No. 10), which aligns it with the side of the spool, then activates the retriever motor by use of a hand switch (No. 6). Within seconds, the tow hook is back to the retriever guide and ready for another launch. Now that's efficient!

● **Hi-Start and Winch-Launch Technique.** One of the most important aspects of hi-start and winch launching is adjusting the location of the glider's tow hook. If this is too far forward, a low, slow launch will result, while having it too far back will result in swerving, uncontrollable tip stalls, and popping off the tow (not necessarily in that order).

I like to start a new glider with the tow hook located about 1/2 to 3/4 inch in front of the CG; that way, the first launch is guaranteed to be at least controllable, if not downright docile, and the tow hook can be moved aft for subsequent launches until the de-

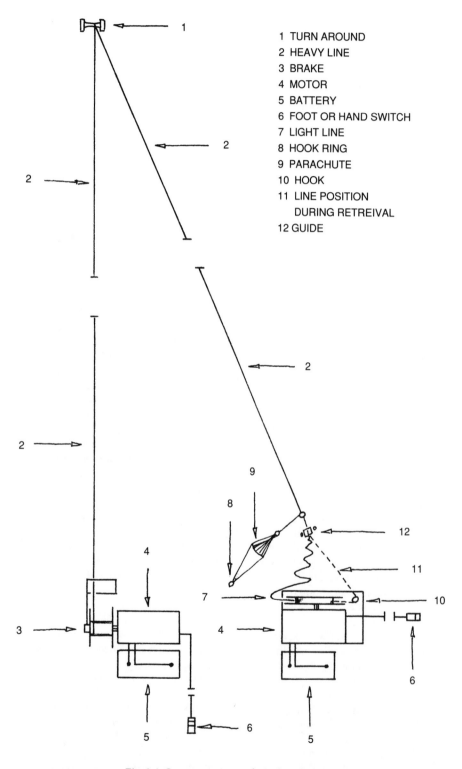

1 TURN AROUND
2 HEAVY LINE
3 BRAKE
4 MOTOR
5 BATTERY
6 FOOT OR HAND SWITCH
7 LIGHT LINE
8 HOOK RING
9 PARACHUTE
10 HOOK
11 LINE POSITION
   DURING RETREIVAL
12 GUIDE

Fig. 6-4: Component parts of winch and retriever.

sired results are obtained. I usually end up with the hook about ¹/₄ inch in front of the CG.

When the tow hook is in the right position, be sure to recheck the wings for equal washout and reset all the control trims to neutral (both transmitter and receiver *are turned on,* aren't they?). This wing and control check is necessary because on tow, the glider will be traveling much faster than its normal glide speed, but very close to a high-speed stall, owing to the increased wing loading imposed by the launching device. As a result, the controls will be *much* more effective than usual, and the slightest trim imbalance will result in *large* deviations from the desired flight path! Now attach the tow ring to the tow hook (be prepared for the tension on the glider if you're using a hi-start), pick up your radio (if you aren't using a neck strap), tap the foot switch a couple of times to put tension on the line (if you're using a winch), and hold the glider with its wings level and the nose elevated at about a 15- to 20-degree attitude. Then smoothly throw the glider forward and upward, taking care to keep the wings level, simultaneously tapping the foot switch if you're winch launching. Remember, the glider must be *thrown* at the start of the launch so that it has enough air flowing over the wings and control surfaces to be flying and controllable; if you let the hi-start or winch merely pull it out of your hand, the wings will be stalled, and things will *really* get out of hand!

At this point, the glider should be going up in a straight line, at a very steep angle, and at high speed. As long as this is the case, stay away from the controls! By all means, be ready to correct any sudden swerves immediately, but be careful not to do anything to cause them. Those using a winch will have to regulate the tension on the line by pulsing the foot switch as the glider rises. Watch the wings carefully, and back off a bit at the first sign of excessive bowing.

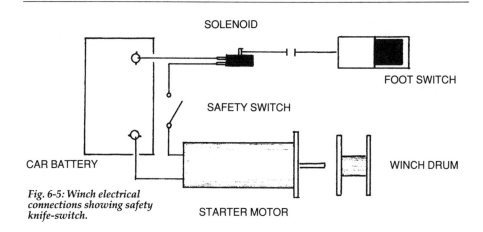

Fig. 6-5: Winch electrical connections showing safety knife-switch.

As long as all is going well, just let the glider fly itself to the apogee of the launch, at which point it will fly itself off the tow. If, for some reason, the glider doesn't break loose from the tow ring by itself, just stab in a little down-elevator to relieve the line tension, and it should fly right off. If you're using a winch, to avoid a backlash on the winch drum, pulse the foot switch once more after the glider releases.

If the glider swerves radically during the launch, it's stalled. Immediately apply some down-elevator to regain flying speed and break the stall, then use rudder and/or ailerons to resume a straight launch path. If you try to recover with rudder and/or ailerons before the stall is broken, the glider will snap roll; use elevator *first!* The primary reasons for stalling the glider during launch are:
- tow hook too far aft
- CG too far aft
- rudder not trimmed neutral
- too much up-elevator trim
- holding too much up-elevator
- not throwing the glider with sufficient force during launch
- launching with one wing low
- launching with the glider at an angle in excess to that of the tow
- too much tension on the winch.
Analyze the situation, correct the problem, and do it right next time!

Once you've achieved nice, stable launches, you should optimize the tow-hook's location. To do this, keep moving the tow hook aft, 1/8 inch at a time, until the glider starts to become slightly squirrelly on launch; this is the point at which it's just nibbling at the edge of a high-speed stall. Move the tow hook about 1/8 inch ahead of this point, and it will be adjusted for the maximum, safe initial angle of climb.

Here are two methods that will assist in gaining maximum-altitude launches:

1. Gradually increase the amount of up-elevator as the climb progresses; this will keep the hi-start stretched out as much and as long as possible, and will ensure the maximum sustained launch angle for either a hi-start or winch launch. Be alert for any sign of imminent stall when doing this, and, if the glider starts to stall or swerves, ease off on the elevator. This technique works better as the wind strength increases.

2. Another method of gaining altitude is the "zoom" launch. Just before reaching the apogee of the launch, and with the tow line still under tension, the glider is made to dive steeply, accelerated by the tension in the line. On reaching maximum speed, abrupt up-elevator is applied, and this results in the glider snapping off the tow and zooming sharply upward at an angle of 45 to 60 degrees. As the glider approaches its stall speed, it's returned to level flight by applying down-elevator.

Winch-launch at the Rose Bowl, Pasadena, CA, and a 100-inch standard-class glider.

While this method does result in a significant altitude gain, its success requires both precise timing and a strong glider.

● **Hand-Launch.** Although popular in Europe, hand-launching is seldom used in the United States. In hand-

To launch, lay the line out to its full length, hook the tow ring to the glider's tow hook, re-check the radios and controls one more time, then signal the towman to start running. When the tension in the line reaches approximately that of a hi-start or

calm, he'll be doing an all-out sprint for the entire launch, but with any kind of wind at all, his job becomes considerably easier. In fact, with a 10-knot breeze, or so, he'll probably have to run *back* toward the pilot during the middle of the launch to avoid

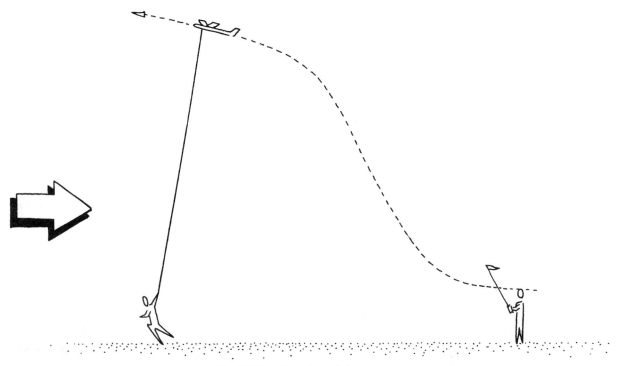

Fig. 6-6: Hand-launching glider.

launching, the main emphasis is on the skill of the towman and not on the pilot. The towman has to be sensitive to the load being placed on the glider at all times in order to regulate the line tension to provide the optimum launch height without over-stressing the glider (Fig.6-6).

The towline most commonly used is a 150-meter length (under a 2-kilo-gram/4.4-pound load, following FAI rules) of 60-pound-test monofilament fishing line. This is affixed to a combination storage reel/tow handle at one end, and has a pennant, swivel, and tow ring attached (in that order) at the other. For ease in winding up the tow line, it helps if the reel is geared.

winch, *throw* the glider straight ahead with wings level and at an upward angle of about 20 degrees. From this point onward, unless the glider swerves or deviates from its course, the pilot *does nothing!* Indeed, if the pilot attempts to steepen the angle with up-elevator, or to increase speed with down-elevator, it will immediately change the line tension felt by the towman. This will cause the towman to speed up or slow down accordingly, thus negating whatever the pilot intended. If the pilot then corrects for the towman's correction, the towman will correct for...well, you get the idea!

Meanwhile, the towman has his work cut out for him. If the wind is

over stressing the glider! As the glider reaches the apogee of the launch, if equipped with a releasable tow hook, it can be released by radio, or the towman can stop, allowing the glider to fly off the tow (perhaps with the help of a little down-elevator by the pilot). A zoom launch is also a possibility. Needless to say, this method of launching requires considerable coordination between towman and pilot, as well as finesse and stamina on the part of the towman.

● **Power Pod.** About the only advantage of this method of launching is that it allows a glider to be launched from a relatively small area, but remember that the glider will have to be *landed* there, too! The disadvantages

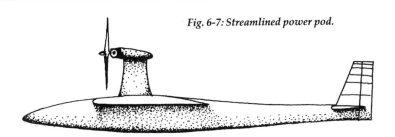

Fig. 6-7: Streamlined power pod.

are the noise, weight, drag and mess associated with liquid-fueled engines, as well as the associated clutter of the accessories necessary to start and run them. For electric power pods, the noise and mess are eliminated, drag stays the same (only if the batteries can be contained in the glider's fuselage, though) and the weight increases significantly. Oh, yes, don't forget a quick charger and an extra servo to switch the motor off. Is it all worth it? *You'll* have to make *that* decision.

If you do want to use a power pod for launching, there are several alternatives available. Figure 6-7 shows the most common type. It has a streamlined engine pod and mounting designed to attach to the top of the wing of a glider, and it's held in place by the rubber bands usually used to attach the wing. A .049 engine is just about right for gliders of the 72- to 100-inch class, and a .09 or .10 works well with larger gliders.

Figure 6-8 shows a plug-in type of pod used primarily on scale, or semi-scale, sailplanes. It's available from United Model Products, and it's adaptable to many different types of gliders and sailplanes. Perhaps the neatest unit of all is shown in Fig. 6-9. This unit fits underneath the glider or sailplane and is held in place by the engine's thrust. When the engine stops, the pod falls off (a short dive and pull-up might be necessary to dislodge it if it's fitted snugly), and it's lowered to earth by a parachute that's contained in the pod and deployed by a

length of very lightweight, breakable thread. The difficulty here, of course, is finding and retrieving the pod wherever it decides to land; also, consider what might happen if it becomes detached while the engine is still running! Whichever type of pod you choose, it should be mounted in such a way that its center of mass is directly over, or under, the glider's CG.

To launch with a power pod, throw the model forward in a level flight attitude and, once it has attained flying speed, initiate a very shallow climb. Don't try to climb steeply, or the glider will stall. Just maintain a steady, shallow climb while circling or flying in a figure-8 pattern (depending on the strength of the wind). Despite the shallow climb attitude, the glider will gain altitude rapidly, so rapidly that you should limit the fuel for the first few flights until you have a feel for how much is required. Gliders have been lost, owing to an engine run that's too long—per-

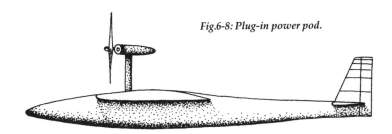

Fig.6-8: Plug-in power pod.

haps abetted by an encounter with a boomer thermal, so keep it short at first!

● **Aero Tow.** Aero towing mimics the full-scale procedure by using a powered airplane to tow a glider or sailplane aloft (Fig. 6-10). This is lots of fun, and a great way to break out of a modeling rut, if you happen to have been caught in one. Aside from excitement and laughs, aero towing provides a real challenge to the building and piloting skills of both participants.

When rigging a glider for aero

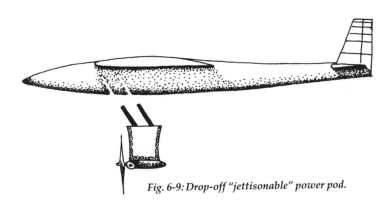

Fig. 6-9: Drop-off "jettisonable" power pod.

Fig. 6-10: Full-scale type of aero tow.

towing, the tow hook should be placed in or on the glider's nose, just as in full-scale operations, and you should be able to release it by operating a servo. The correct vertical placement of the tow line is in line with the glider's CG, which will generally be fairly high on the fuselage. The towing line should be of non-stretchable material (40-pound test Dacron squidding line is a good choice) and about 100 feet long.

As for the tug (as airplanes that tow gliders are called), it can be rigged with the tow connection at the tail, as in full-scale practice. This can, however, create a great deal of excitement, as a glider that's flown less than skillfully can jerk the tug all over the sky. Of course, this is true of full-scale operations, too! A more docile location for the tug's tow hook is on a pylon extending several inches above the tug's CG, i.e., high enough for the tow line to clear the tug's tail when the glider is in its proper position, which in this case is above the tug (Fig 6-11). (The opposite would be true if the pylon or hook were beneath the tug.) Experiment to discover what type of rigging works best for you.

When launching with an aero tow, face the tug and glider into the wind with the tow line stretched fully between them. Now, add a little power to the tug to get the glider rolling, then give it full throttle. The glider will become airborne before the tug does, and it should take up a position about 5 or 6 feet above the tug. After the tug has lifted off, it should start making very shallow climbing turns, the glider following about 20 feet above the tug and slightly outside the circumference of the tug's turn. Upon

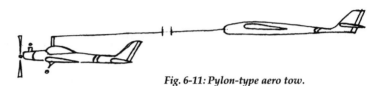

Fig. 6-11: Pylon-type aero tow.

reaching the desired altitude, simply activate the glider's release; in full-scale practice, the tug dives to the left, the glider breaks right, and now you're soaring!

What's a Thermal

Thermals are formed as a result of differential heating of the earth's surface. The most common heat source for thermal production is the sun, although some man-made sources, such as a heated chicken shed in winter, or a steel mill almost any time, can produce thermal activity that's useful to model glider pilots. For the moment, let's consider only the effects of the sun.

As the sun shines on the earth's surface, different areas absorb the radiant energy it provides at different rates. As a particularly heat-absorbent area warms, it transfers its heat to the air above it, which begins to rise. As this air from the warmed area rises, cooler air from the surrounding terrain flows in to replace it, and this is, in turn, heated so that it rises aloft (Fig. 6-12). In the absence of wind, this heated air will be carried aloft in a vertical column that continues to rise and expand until its temperature is reduced to that of the surrounding air. If the air is sufficiently humid, this expansional cooling will lower the temperature to the dew point and

a cloud will be formed. In any case, this now-cooled air will start flowing downward to replace the cool surface air flowing into the thermal, which is in turn being heated and is replacing the hotter air being carried aloft. Since, on a large scale, the areas producing thermals will be only a small proportion of the total area, the up-drafts, or lift, in the thermals will be much stronger than the downdrafts, or sink, in the surrounding area. This process will continue until something like wind, or a cloud's shadow on the ground, interrupts the heat source.

A thermal rising in a continuous column (as already described) is called a chimney thermal, and in the presence of strong, continuous heating, it's the most prevalent type. However, the presence of wind or a cloud shadow might cool the heat-producing surface sufficiently to slow, or even halt, the convective, thermal-producing process, which will begin anew as soon as the former conditions are restored. This process will produce "bubbles" of rising air, known as bubble thermals, and they can vary tremendously in size (Fig. 6-13). In the presence of continuous heating, bubble thermals can also be formed by a strong wind pulling, or shearing, the chimney thermal into smaller, irregularly shaped bubbles. Present theory holds that, if large enough, bubble thermals assume the

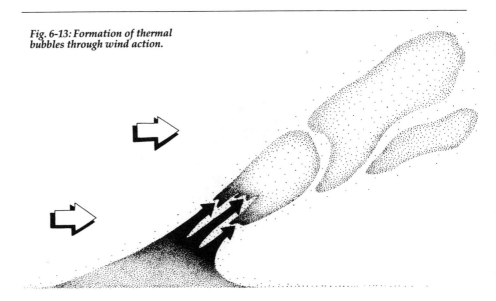

Fig. 6-13: Formation of thermal bubbles through wind action.

form of a vortex shell, with strong lift at the center and only weak, or no, lift at the edges (Fig. 6-14). Of course, just as a chimney thermal "leans" away from the wind, bubble thermals will drift downwind as they rise.

Upslope Convection

There's one more useful type of lift caused by thermal convective activity, but it doesn't produce thermals in the classic sense. Upslope convection is created when the sun heats the bottom and side(s) of a deep valley (we're talking thousands of feet here) and thus causes the air to expand and rise (Fig. 6-15). If there's sufficient heating of the valley's sides, the air will flow up the slope and be replaced by cooler air flowing in from the ends of the valley. In the absence of atmospheric winds, this rising air can create an impressive amount of lift. Be aware that there may be downdrafts at the center of the valley.

Wave Lift

Wave lift is another type of lift that's useful to the thermal glider pilot. As wind flows over obstructions, such as a line of mountains or hills, it's forced to rise on the windward side (creating slope lift) and becomes compressed against the smoother air

above. On the lee side of the obstruction, the wind descends toward the surface where it again becomes compressed and is forced to rise, again becoming compressed against the stable air above, whence it descends. On a large scale, such waves have been known to continue for hundreds of miles downwind of mountain ranges, such as the Sierras or Rockies, and have created lift to 45,000 feet and more! Obviously, lift on this scale is useless to model gliders, but that produced by smaller obstructions, such as hills, levees, and even irrigation ditches is most useful.

To fly in wave lift, bear in mind that waves run parallel to the line of obstructions, they are stationary, and the maximum lift will be on the upwind side and top of the wave. Since small-scale waves are invisible (large waves are often marked by standing lenticular clouds), your first clue as to their existence will be on launching or flying into sustained lift or sink. In either case, flying upwind and downwind will soon reveal the area of optimum lift, and you can make the most of it by flying crosswind in that area. Be alert to the possibility of wave lift while you're flying, and you might find yourself flying while others are on the ground!

Fig. 6-12: Cooler air flows inward, is heated and rises aloft.

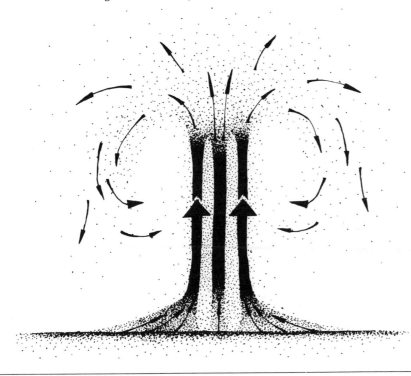

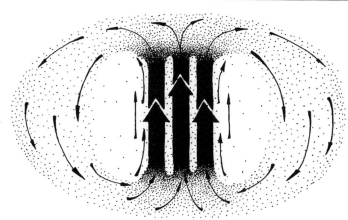

Fig. 6-14: Vortex shell form of individual bubble thermal.

Locating Thermals

As you know, in level flight, a glider is always descending in relation to the surrounding air. Obviously then, the only way to sustain flight beyond the sink time in still air (other than using a motor) is to fly in air that's rising at a rate that's greater than, or at least equal to, that at which the glider is sinking. Therefore, as glider pilots, our goal is to maximize the time spent in thermal lift, and minimize that spent in the surrounding "sink." Our first step toward realizing that goal is recognizing the areas that are most likely to produce lift.

The strongest thermals will occur where there's the greatest amount of sustained *differential* heating; heated air will rise in proportion to the difference in temperature between it and the surrounding air. We're looking for heat-absorbent areas that are next to less absorbent areas. Since the least heat-absorbent areas will probably have the greatest downdrafts, these are the areas we should avoid. Good examples of thermal-producing terrain are blacktop parking lots, industrial and shopping centers, housing tracts, areas with crops, sand or dry lakes. Poor areas include lakes or ponds, woods, ploughed fields and pasture land. On a smaller level, a heat-absorbent area immediately in the lee of a man-made or natural windbreak will be warmer than the surrounding wind-cooled terrain. Conversely, an area shaded by a barn, for example, will be cooler than the surrounding terrain (or the barn's roof, for that matter).

While thermals are invisible, they can often be detected by "feel," or by the presence of hawks, gulls, or other birds soaring in them. If you're

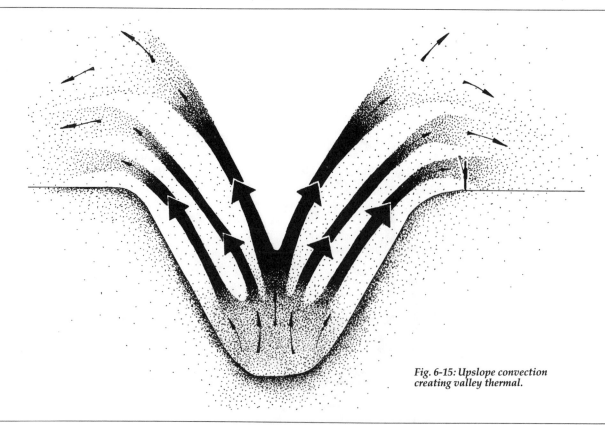

Fig. 6-15: Upslope convection creating valley thermal.

standing in a field and suddenly feel a light breeze of warmer air, you've just detected a thermal. On a day with a light, constant breeze, a change in the direction or strength of the breeze probably indicates air flowing into a thermal, and you can take advantage of this by flying in the direction of the wind's shift to find the thermal.

Keeping these points in mind will greatly assist you in choosing, and making the most of, a thermal soaring site. As you gain experience, you'll rapidly develop the uncanny ability to "read" an unfamiliar flying site.

Flying in Thermals

Once our glider has been launched, the first order of business is to find some lift and gain more altitude, but first, we need to formulate a strategy for doing so and to learn to recognize the clues the glider provides when it's being affected by lift or sink.

As you'll recall from the section on thermal development, the total area of sinking air is far larger than the area of air rising in thermals. Fortunately for us, however, the rising air is going up at a much faster rate than the surrounding air, or sink, is descending. Obviously, we need to maximize our time in the rising air and minimize that spent in sinking air. Our basic strategy, therefore, is to fly fast while in sink to cover as much area as possible while looking for lift, and to fly

Open-class glider in flight.

slowly while in lift to maximize our altitude gain. Further, we want to carefully observe the glider for any deviation from its expected flight performance, because this is our best indication of the external forces acting upon it.

Let's assume, for example, that we're launching from a large grassy area with a blacktop parking lot to our right, a small pond upwind in front of us, and a row of metal-roofed buildings running along the left bank of the pond. To our rear and downwind is a forest. Drawing upon our knowledge of thermal formation, we

can expect to find lift over, and/or slightly downwind of, the parking lot and the buildings, with an area of sink expected over the pond, as well as over the trees. Since the parking lot is larger and closer than the buildings, look for lift there first. As the glider climbs skyward on launch, carefully watch its attitude for any unexpected changes; a slight nose-up or down, or a wing flipping up or down without control inputs probably indicates the presence of a thermal. Be alert for these indications while on tow; many people dismiss them as radio "glitches" and then wonder why they can never find lift when everyone else is struggling to keep their gliders in sight! For the sake of our example, however, assume that our launch was perfectly normal.

As we release from the tow, make a turn to the right and head for the area over the parking lot, trimming the glider to a moderately fast and stable speed, i.e., one that will permit the glider to cover the greatest distance from any given altitude. This speed is known as maximum L/D (lift/drag). We find nothing special directly over the parking lot, but,

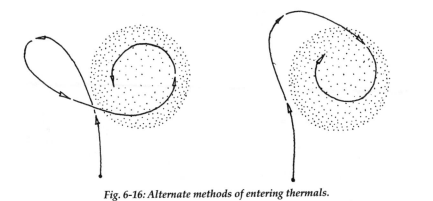

Fig. 6-16: Alternate methods of entering thermals.

A 12V power winch.

since a light breeze is blowing, we decide to continue downwind to see if a thermal is lurking there. Sure enough, the right wing flips up abruptly and the glider tries to turn to the left; we've just found the edge of a thermal!

There are two methods for entering the thermal (Fig. 6-16), which we know is to our right. One method that generally works best for large, slow-turning gliders, is to continue the thermal-induced turn for 270 degrees to the left and to enter the thermal at a right angle to the original course. The other method (which I usually prefer) is to make a fairly wide 180-degree turn back into the thermal, which, in this case, is to the right. Whichever method is chosen, once in the thermal, we'll need to start circling tightly, while slowing the glider to a speed that will permit the maximum amount of time aloft from a given altitude. This is known as minimum sink speed, and this speed is just slightly above the stall.

Assume that our glider is going up at a fairly good rate. The goal now is not just to stay in the thermal, but to find and fly in the best lift in that thermal. Since there's a slight breeze present for our example, assume that the thermal will drift downwind and that we should plan our circling so as to follow it. In addition, we'll need to carefully monitor the speed and climb rate of

our glider (pitch and bank attitudes are good indicators of any lift changes while circling) and adjust our circling for optimum use of the available lift. With careful observation and some experimentation, you'll be amazed at how rapidly you'll develop a feel for staying in the center of a thermal. Of course, this can lead to other problems, such as determining when and how to get out of them! (More about that later.)

For this example, we recognize that our glider has gained so much altitude that it's in danger of disappearing, and if we continue to fol-

low the thermal downwind and lose the lift, we'll then be in the sink over the trees and perhaps unable to glide back upwind to a safe landing on the field. Being smart, we turn the airplane upwind to escape the thermal and trim to maximum L/D speed so that we're able to travel the greatest distance from our altitude.

Suddenly, the glider picks up ground speed and starts to sink rapidly; it has encountered a strong downdraft at the edge of the thermal! Recalling that we need to minimize the amount of time spent in sink, we trim for a speed that will get us out of the sink fast and moving upwind rapidly (best penetration speed). We're soon out of the heavy sink adjoining the thermal. We then re-trim to maximum L/D and head for the metal buildings, where we expect to find lift once again, and where we can glide to a safe landing if we're unsuccessful.

As we approach the area just downwind of the metal buildings, the glider dips, then noses up sharply and stalls. This is a good indication that the glider has just flown straight into a strong thermal, and the best tactic in this case is to recover from the stall straight ahead into the thermal and

A 12V power-line retriever.

start to circle. An alternative is to recover and fly straight *through* the thermal, then make a 270-degree turn to re-enter the thermal at a 90-degree angle to the original course. The theory is that this helps to pinpoint the center of the thermal, but why waste the time and risk being caught in sink instead? I recommend that you recover and start to circle immediately. The center of the thermal can thus be sought, while the glider is gaining altitude in lift.

So here we are, ascending in a thermal once again! Since this thermal is being produced by the heating of the buildings' roofs, we should anticipate that this thermal will be smaller and produce less lift than that over the parking lot. Our goal here is to gain sufficient altitude to return to the known "boomer" working over the parking lot, where we can be carried even further aloft and obtain altitude for aerobatics, or further exploration of the surrounding area. Flying back and forth between the two areas a few times will rapidly reveal how this flying site is working, and allow us to very accurately predict the location and strength of the available lift.

Escaping a Runaway Thermal

Don't laugh! Getting caught in a thermal and losing sight of your glider is a serious problem. Since it *is* a possibility, be sure your name, address and telephone number are somewhere in, or on, your glider. Whenever the wingspan of your glider appears to be less than the width of your thumb when you hold out your thumb in front of it at arm's length, it's time to leave the thermal. Since thermals expand as they rise, this might not be as easy as you think. First, try to fly upwind and out of the thermal. If that doesn't work, place the glider in a shallow dive, but guard against gaining excessive air speed. It's difficult to judge air speed at a distance, and if you dive too fast, you could cause the glider to break apart. Try consecutive loops with a long downside. If the glider is still being carried aloft, you

have no choice: Slow the glider to stall it, pull the stick all the way back, and push it all the way to the right or left. Hold those inputs and spin down. A spin places very low stress upon your glider and will rapidly get it down to a safe altitude.

Landing

One of the nice things about thermal soaring is that since a large area is necessary for launching, it follows that a large area will also be available

A 12V power-line retriever.

for landing. Ironically, with huge amounts of real estate available for landing (compared with what's usually available at a slope site), thermal pilots put a great deal of emphasis on making *spot landings,* especially in contests. This being the case, let's discuss what's involved in making precise landings.

Obviously, it's best to land *into* the wind, since the glider's ground speed will be at a minimum in that condition. Therefore, pick a landing site well upwind of any obstructions and stand about 30 feet upwind of it. Now circle your glider 100 yards or so upwind of your position.

The key to precise landings is consistency, and you need to establish a

landing pattern that you can use every time. I recommend a U-shaped pattern consisting of downwind, base (when the glider is flying crosswind) and final (flying into the wind) legs. Establish a key point directly abeam of your position on the downwind leg across which you'll always fly your glider at the same distance, altitude and air speed (judged by the glider's attitude)—generally, about one-third faster than stall speed. For what it's worth, I usually pick a key point that's 75 feet abeam of my position

and 50 feet high.

With your landing site, pattern and key point established, circle your glider down to an altitude that allows it to reach the key point at approach air speed, and head for the key point. For your first attempt, cross the key point and continue downwind for what seems a reasonable distance, then turn the glider across the wind onto the base leg. Roll out of that turn and then into another, positioning the glider so that it's directly downwind of the landing spot and coming straight at you (some pilots prefer to stand slightly to one side). Now slow the glider to a speed just above stall and wait.

You'll notice that, as the glider

sinks to within its wingspan distance above the ground, it will tend to float and extend its glide. This phenomenon is called ground effect, and it's caused by a decrease in induced drag. Ignore it, and maintain the glider's air speed just above stall until it touches down.

If the glider overshoots the landing spot, you'll have to extend the downwind leg by half the distance it overshot. If it landed short, decrease the length of the downwind leg similarly. Make a mental note of the correction, then try it again. You'll soon be consistently landing on, or very near, your chosen spot!

Of course, there's still a variable in the equation, and that variable is the wind speed. Varying wind speed is compensated for by varying the length of the downwind leg. In still air, the length of the downwind leg will be at its maximum; as the wind speed increases, you'll have to shorten the downwind leg accordingly.

There's also an interesting constant in the landing equation: time. As long as you're consistent in your arrival at the key point, flying your pattern and turns, and managing your air speed, the time measured from crossing the key point until the glider touches down will remain constant. This is of great importance to the contest glider guider who, in addition to making a spot landing, is also expected to land at a precise time after tow release!

Pilot's briefing before a thermal contest.

Thermal Contests

There are two basic types of thermal contests: precision duration and total duration. In a precision-duration contest, pilots are asked to make a flight of exact duration; usually 2, 5, 7, or ten minutes, depending on the conditions determined by the contest director. Timing starts when the glider is released from the tow, and it ends when the glider first touches the ground (or a ground-based object, like that glider-grabbing tree). In addition, the pilot must land the glider within a 25-foot landing circle with its nose as close as possible to a spot in the center. Points are subtracted by the second for missing the precise duration assigned and awarded for proximity to the landing spot.

When landing, if the glider turns over, sheds parts, or is damaged so it

can't be flown without repair, all landing points are lost. In this type of contest, if conditions permit, contestants usually fly three rounds, each of a different assigned duration.

In a total-duration contest, pilots have to make three flights totalling exactly 15 minutes, and none may be longer than 7 minutes. As with the precision-duration contest, each flight ends with a spot landing, and points are awarded in the same way.

To make the competition fair for all, gliders generally compete only with others of the same class. The classes are:

Class A: Gliders with a wingspan of 1 1/2 meters, or less.
2-Meter Class: Gliders with a wingspan of 2 meters, or less; unlimited controls.
Standard Class: Gliders with a wingspan of 100 inches, or less; rudder and elevator controls only.
Modified Standard Class: Gliders with a wingspan of 100 inches, or less; unlimited controls.
Open Class: Gliders with a wingspan of more than 100 inches; unlimited controls.

Because thermal contests can be held almost anywhere, have enough space and are relatively immune to weather conditions, they're very popular, and contests are available from the local club level to the national championship level. Almost all contests are run according to the rules of the Academy of Model

Spot-landing with pilot, timer, and judge.

Aeronautics, and an AMA membership card is usually required to enter. Membership includes $1,000,000 liability insurance coverage and affords many other valuable benefits. Every R/C pilot should join and support this fine organization.

F3B Multi-Task Competition

Because it's so different, F3B is listed separately from other thermal competition. It's a highly specialized international game for very experienced pilots. Because of the large number of *national* egos involved, F3B rules change frequently, so I'll discuss the tasks only in a general manner. Anyone seriously interested in F3B competition should get a current rule book from the AMA.

In F3B contests, pilots are assigned multiple tasks of duration, distance and speed. The duration task consists of a set time within which the pilot is allowed unlimited attempts to obtain as many points as possible in a single flight, at a rate of one point per second aloft, up to a fixed maximum that's less than the set time. For example: 9 minutes is allowed in which to accumulate a maximum of 360 points (6 minutes). If more than one flight is made, only the last one is scored, and one point per second is deducted for exceeding the allowed times. Bonus points are awarded for spot landings.

The distance task is somewhat similar to a pylon race, although a buzzer located next to the pilot signals the glider's passing of the markers, of which there are two. The goal is to complete as many laps of the course as possible within a fixed time, which is now 4 minutes. The glider must land within the course lines within the fixed time, and partial laps completed are counted to the nearest quarter-lap behind the glider's final position.

For the speed task, a closed course is established, the goal being to fly through the start gate, around the far marker and back through the start

gate in the shortest time. Again, marker passing is signaled by a buzzer. The pilot is allowed unlimited launches in a 4-minute period, but once the course has been entered, the only allowable record run has begun. Landing within the course zeros the task.

All tasks are flown a minimum of two rounds, and a score is compiled from the results.

L.S.F. Achievement Tasks

For those wishing to measure their soaring achievement against established norms without entering all-out competition, the League of Silent Flight has devised a series of five tasks of progressively increasing difficulty. For Level 1, the pilot must make either two thermal

flights lasting 5 minutes, or one 5-minute thermal flight and one 15-minute slope flight. In each case, the landing must be within 200 meters of the launch point. In addition, five spot landings within 3 meters of a designated spot must be made. Any adult or Level I pilot who isn't

Everyone has a different spot-landing style!

a relative may witness and sign off your flights.

After achieving Level 1, the going gets increasingly tough, and very few pilots have achieved Level V status. Perhaps it's just the challenge you're looking for! To obtain information and forms, send $1 to League of Silent Flight.

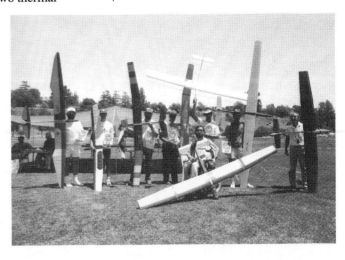

Pasadena Soaring Society Contest. Winners pose proudly with their gliders after contest.

Sometimes this is the only way to get 'em down!

Slope Soaring

One of the great delights of slope soaring is the ease with which we can carry the equipment; all we need is a glider and a radio. No hi-start or winch for *us;* to launch, all we have to do is throw our glider from the top of a hill or cliff toward which the wind is blowing, and we're flying! On most days, it's possible to stay aloft as long as the batteries hold out, or until someone else wants the frequency, and it's easy to gain altitude for repeated sequences of aerobatics. To top it off, the view is usually extraordinary from our lofty vantage point.

Flying wing soars over the city.

Selecting a Slope-Soaring Site

While thermal soaring can be practiced just about anywhere, a suitable slope-soaring site isn't always available. Actually, it's amazing how little slope it takes to provide adequate lift for a model sailplane, and many thermal soaring sites have areas where at least some slope lift is available when the wind is blowing, if you know where to look. For now, however, let's consider the qualities of an ideal slope-soaring location.

Most important, obviously, is the existence of a slope, cliff, or bowl, preferably somewhere between absolutely vertical and about 45 degrees, at least several hundred feet high and several hundred feet long, facing directly into the prevailing wind. This slope should have a large (we're talking *miles* here), unobstructed flat area leading from its base directly upwind of it so that the air is as smooth and as undisturbed by turbulence as possible. Additionally, our slope should be open to the public, and it should have a road conveniently leading to a parking area at the top which, as long as we're dreaming, should be devoid of buildings, fences, telephone poles and wires, radio towers and other sundry impedimenta. It would be really great if this slope were also cushioned by nice, soft, tall grass with a broad, flat grassy landing area located at the top. Hey, let's add an elevator leading to a hobby shop and fully equipped model airplane repair center, and a soda fountain, a bar/restaurant...oops, back to reality! Have you *ever* found a soaring site like this? Well, I haven't either, although some come awfully close— except for the amenities, of course!

A good example is found at Torrey Pines near San Diego, CA. At Torrey Pines, the wind blows steadily and uninterrupted for thousands of miles

Hand-launching a slope glider.

across the Pacific Ocean, finally reaching the several-hundred-foot-high vertical cliffs and creating fabulous slope-soaring conditions. Unfortunately, full-scale gliders and hang-gliders also find these conditions irresistible, so it can get somewhat crowded at times.

Many other great soaring sites can be found along the coast, and not just the Pacific Coast; there's great soaring at the dunes on the west coast of Michigan, Sleeping Bear Dunes being the most well-known. Many amazingly small lakes afford excellent slope soaring along their downwind shores. Many inland areas also have outstanding sites, often featuring thermal activity in addition to the slope lift; I have the good fortune to have one such site within 1/4 mile of my home in Los Angeles!

While we'd all like to have an ideal slope nearby, some who live in the flatter areas of the country will have to make do with less-than-ideal conditions or take up thermal soaring, which is lots of fun, too! You should know, though, that it's possible to find slope lift (not great, but "flyable") near ditches and river em-

bankments, long buildings and solid-fence rows. Even if incapable of sustaining dramatic slope soaring, these sources of lift can be most helpful to thermal glider guiders. Keep the above characteristics in mind, and look around you carefully; I'm sure you'll find many more areas with slope-soaring potential than you previously thought existed.

Launching

At first glance, launching a glider from the slope seems ridiculously simple; just throw it off and fly! While it *is* just about that easy, there are a few things to consider before, during and after launch that will greatly improve your flying.

To begin with, think about where you're going to land! This seems obvious, but I've watched several accomplished thermal soaring pilots (who were used to landing on the football field they launched from) pitch their gliders into the blue without giving landing the slightest thought. Since most slope-soaring sites have pretty rugged topographical characteristics with rather small and/or difficult landing areas (some

have none: you *catch* your plane in your hand), this usually results in our hero's trying to fly a plane in front of him while simultaneously attempting to reconnoiter the terrain behind him for a suitable landing site. The situation usually ends with an "assist" from a local flier, or a broken plane, if the newcomer is too proud to ask for help!

The next thing to consider is the wind: Is it too little, too much, or just about right for your glider? The best way to evaluate this is to stand at the lip of the slope while holding your glider aloft in a level flight attitude. If the glider develops enough lift to all but lift you along with it, consider either adding ballast (lots of ballast!) to it, or putting it back in the car. If, on the other hand, it just sits there with no appreciable lift, there's probably not enough wind to fly that particular glider. The ideal situation is to feel a definite lifting sensation somewhere between these two extremes.

Finally, evaluate the flying site carefully, "reading" the areas of best lift and probable sink, rotors, etc., and plan where and how you'll fly once your glider is in the air. There's more about this in the next section. Also, note the positions of other pilots and spectators, planning your launch and flight so as to maintain a safe distance from them. You might check their frequency flags while you're at it! Having considered all these factors, you're now ready to launch. Be sure to turn on the radios! If you're right-handed, I suggest that you launch while holding the radio in your left hand with your thumb on the right stick and your fingers wrapped over the top of the transmitter, the antenna extending between your middle and ring fingers. Pick up the glider with your right hand at the CG and hold it aloft, feeling for the lift and checking the radio operation and control deflections. When you're ready, center the controls and throw the glider forward and slightly downward directly into the wind, taking care to release it perfectly straight.

Now, simply move your right hand over to the radio and enjoy the flight!

Flying: Slope-Soaring Basics

For the moment, let's assume that our slope is perfectly even in height and length, with no obstructions or variations of any kind, thus creating smooth and even lift across its face. Let's further assume that the wind is steadily blowing directly into the slope.

Given these conditions, the best technique after launching is to fly directly out from the slope for some distance (the air will be smoother there) and then to initiate a shallow turn one way or the other, levelling off to fly along, or above, the rim. Our goal is to keep the glider an equal distance from the rim while flying along its length. To do this, the

(away from the slope), will allow the glider to climb as high as the lift on our example slope will allow. In very light winds, flying this classic figure-8 pattern as close to the rim of the slope as possible might be the only way to sustain flight (Fig. 7-2).

There are two reasons for making all turns into the wind and away from the hill:
● Since the glider must be crabbed into the wind to maintain its track across the hill, it will have to make less of a turn to reverse its direction. That is, if the glider requires a crab angle of 15 degrees into the wind, it can reverse direction by making a 150-degree turn into the wind, whereas it will require a 210-degree turn away from the wind to accomplish the same course reversal.
● The other reason for making all turns into the wind is that the glider's

ground speed will be slower than if the turns were made with the wind. This will help us to avoid being blown downwind of the rim of the slope while making a turn and ending up in downdrafts, or the frequently terminal turbulence of the back-slope "rotor."

To better understand what happens if a glider flies behind the rim of the slope, consider the forces acting to create lift and how they must eventually be dispersed. Referring to Fig. 7-3, it's clear that wind blowing toward the hill at the lower levels encounters the solid ground and is forced to deviate upward, following the contour of the slope. Wind moving toward the slope at higher levels can't blow directly upon the slope but, instead, bumps into the air rushing up from below, thereby being forced upward itself and compressing the already rising air in the process. By visualizing the wind approaching the slope as a number of layers, each pressing on and being diverted by the layer below it, it's easy to see that a cushion of air is built up for some distance in front of the slope and for quite a distance above it as well. This is why the smoothest air will be found well in front of the slope where the cushioning effect is the greatest.

But what happens when the rising compressed air reaches the top of the slope? Referring again to the illustration, it can be seen that the bottom layer of air will attempt to follow the ground's contour, while the layers above will be forced upward, well

Fig. 7-1: Glider crabbing into wind in order to maintain a straight flight path.

glider must compensate for the wind's tendency to blow it sideways by "crabbing" across the slope, i.e., the glider's nose must be pointed slightly into the wind for it to fly a straight path parallel to the length of the slope (Fig. 7-1). Once the glider has flown as far away as you wish it to go, a shallow turn *into the wind* should be initiated and the aircraft flown back in the other direction.

Repeating this sequence, taking care to make all turns into the wind

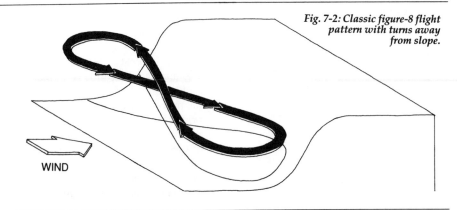

Fig. 7-2: Classic figure-8 flight pattern with turns away from slope.

WIND

above the crest of the slope. This area, well above the crest, is generally the area of greatest and highest lift, and it's usually the preferred location for maximum altitude gain. However, the situation is complicated by the fact that the air in front of the slope is compressed more than the air behind it, and as the air flows over the top, it tries to equalize this pressure differential by expanding. Since the only way for it to expand is downward (remember the compressed layers above), it initiates a sort of downward rolling and tumbling pattern that's

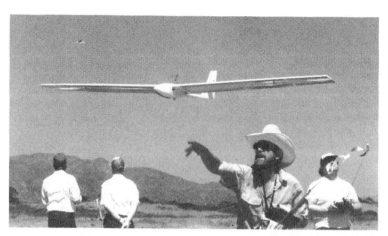

Launching Accipiter, note tipperons.

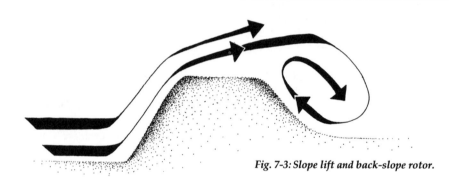

Fig. 7-3: Slope lift and back-slope rotor.

called a rotor. This rotor can extend for a surprising distance behind the hill and can, given sufficient wind strength, generate enough violent turbulence to cause a glider to break up in flight! At the very least, a glider caught in the rotor will be difficult, if not impossible, to control. The best policy to pursue with regard to rotors is to avoid them altogether; don't fly, or get blown, over the back of the hill!

Now that you understand how slope lift is generated and are aware of the existence and location of the rotor, it will be easier to put the mechanics of that lift to work for you. Generally speaking, the further upwind and/or down slope you fly, the less lift will be available, eventually reaching a point at which flight cannot be sustained. Many unintentional landings are made this way! Conversely, the most lift will be found close to the

slope and above the rim, but keep fully in mind the dangers of the rotor lurking just downwind. Utilizing the basic figure-8 pattern and taking care to make all turns into the wind (at least for a while), explore the lift dynamics of your slope by flying your glider high and low, near and far, until you have a firm grasp of the practical application of these principles.

Getting the Most out of a Site

Of course, most slope-soaring sites will differ significantly from the highly simplified example used in the previous section, but the basic principles will remain the same. To illustrate the practical application of these principles to a real slope under a number of different conditions, let's consider a relatively complicated site that's subject to

winds from two basic directions.

Figure 7-4 is a non-scale, simplified representation of an actual slope site near my home—let's call it Kite Hill. Facing southwest, Kite Hill rises about 800 feet above the housing and industrial areas, railroad yards, and freeway that extend outward from its base for several miles, thus allowing it to develop excellent slope lift from the usual prevailing westerly wind. The areas below it also produce some thermal activity, which I'll discuss in detail a little later. For now, visualize a westerly wind quartering in from the upper right, and take a few moments to study Fig. 7-4, applying the basic principles of slope-lift generation discussed in the previous section.

Now refer to Fig. 7-5. Obviously, with the west-wind condition depicted, the area of maximum lift will be found within and along the rim of the bowl at area B and, as you might expect, most flying is done in this bowl and along the rim of the hill toward the west-northwest. Considerable lift is also found off the end of the point of ridge A, although it's tricky to fly in this area, because the point is fairly small and tends to split the wind. The rotor at the back of ridge A is right where we would expect it to be, but not so obvious is the rotor shown next to the descending ridge D. Actually, a glider flown at or above the rim of the hill will never encounter this rotor, because it's formed along the ridge line about 100 feet below the rim, although its effect is evident, if a glider is flown just below the rim at this point.

It's always interesting to observe pilots who are unfamiliar with the conditions at Kite Hill: They'll start by flying along and above the rim, traversing back and forth until they've gained sufficient altitude to dive into the bowl and perform some aerobatics, then climbing along the rim to repeat the process. Eventually, they drop so far into the bowl that, during the subsequent climb-out, they pass ridge D at an altitude below the rim, and this results in the most incredible aerial gyrations imaginable. All this is invariably accompanied by a great deal of urgent, animated screaming about "radio hits" and "who's on my frequency?" Many find it difficult to accept that their problem was caused by flying through a rotor and severe wind shear, until it's demonstrated that the "radio interference" is *always* present in that location!

Actually, there's another place along the rim where wind shear (the rapid change in speed and/or direction of the wind) is likely to exist.

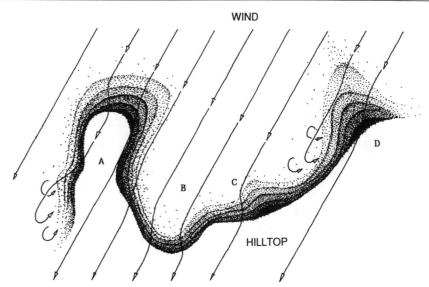

Fig. 7-5: Kite Hill with wind blowing from west.

Have you spotted it yet? That's right; there's a small area to the left of ridge C where more than one pilot has complained of a "radio glitch," but now *you* know better, right?

Finally, note the northwest face of ridge A. Here, the wind parallels the rim and forms a relatively "dead" area. Any shift of the wind toward the south, no matter how slight it

might be or how short its duration, will create a very strong shear. It pays to avoid areas such as this if the wind is gusty and shifting.

Speaking of shifting, it's not uncommon at Kite Hill, especially in the summertime, for the prevailing wind to shift to the south for a day or more. Figure 7-6 shows how the hill "works" under this condition. At these times, the bowl area northwest of ridge A is home to a *very* healthy rotor. Fortunately, the edge of the bowl rises at point B and creates a small pocket of relatively dead air with no shear—but also no lift. I say fortunately, because this is the best (softest) landing site on the hill!

Any time you fly from a slope located downwind a mile or more of ground, buildings, parking lots, or other areas capable of absorbing solar heat, you're likely to experience thermal activity along with the slope lift. This synergistic bonus can add tremendous excitement to your slope soaring, permitting altitude gains bordering on the ridiculous and allowing fantastic sequences of linked aerobatics on the way down! Fortunately, Kite Hill benefits frequently from these conditions, and on such days, the flying is unparalleled!

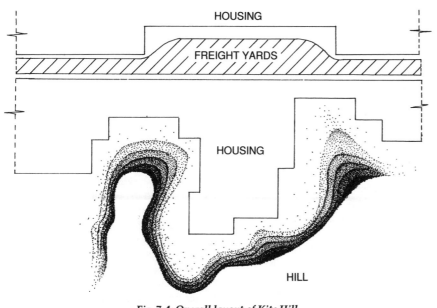

Fig. 7-4: Overall layout of Kite Hill.

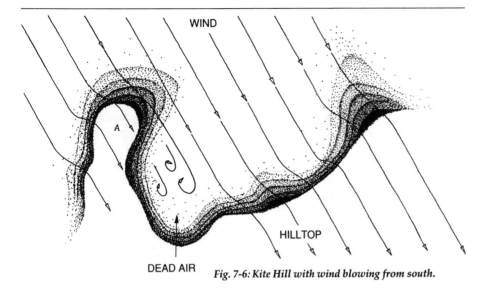

WIND

A

HILLTOP

DEAD AIR

Fig. 7-6: Kite Hill with wind blowing from south.

Given a clear frequency, it's possible to fly until the batteries quit while performing every maneuver you've ever heard of (and some you haven't), and as for altitude and distance, well…just make sure your name, address and phone number are in your glider!

For more information about thermals in general: what they are, how they develop, and how best to make use of them, please refer to the chapter on Thermal Soaring. Assuming that you've read that chapter, or that you already have that knowledge, let's take a look at the specific thermal-generating conditions affecting Kite Hill and how they affect us.

Referring to Fig. 7-7, the central housing area is obviously a prime thermal generator and, given the prevailing westerly wind, most of its lift will be found in the main bowl, at position B. Because thermal "bubbles" are broken loose from the surface by the wind, very little thermal activity will be found directly over the housing area itself; the thermals found there are quite randomly distributed and certainly can't be predicted or depended upon. This is a bad place to "go hunting"!

The housing area to the right of the illustration is actually larger than the area depicted in the center, and it pro-

duces a tremendous amount of very consistent lift over the long, sloping ridge at position C. This is actually the best lift-producing location on the hill—much better than over the main bowl at B! Why? The thermal bubbles blown into the main bowl meet violently rising air blowing up a steep, irregular canyon; this rising air literally shreds the thermals into pieces too small to circle in, although they do generate a significant amount of additional lift in this area. This effect is especially conspicuous by its absence on cold, overcast days. On the other hand, the thermals found above ridge C have been guided up a very long, smooth, gently sloping ridge where the wind impacts the slope and climbs it much more gently. This area is a consistent producer of "boomer" thermals; it's a great place to *really* range-test your glider, as well as your nerve!

Another great thermal-producing area is the freight yards—a huge area made up primarily of black ballast stones. While it would seem that thermals generated there would miss Kite Hill entirely, this is not quite the case. While some of them do, indeed, miss the hill, many of those thermals form a convenient line of lift between the freight yard and the point of the ridge at position A, meeting the ridge about

halfway up, where its slope is relatively gentle. While this area doesn't produce thermal lift as awesome and consistent as that found at C, the lift does extend considerably further from the slope, that distance being inversely proportional to the strength of the wind, of course. On a sunny day with the wind blowing steadily from the west at about 10 to 15 knots, it's entirely feasible to fly endlessly in huge circles from ridge C far out over the housing area, then to ridge A, and back along the rim of the main bowl to ridge C. Those feeling really bold do it the *opposite* way. Do you understand why that would be more difficult? I'll wait for your answer while you analyze the situation…

Wow! That sure didn't take long! You're right: From ridge A out over the housing, you're starting at a lower altitude than at C and proceeding along a descending line of thermals toward the freight yards, then flying upwind through an area with no predictable lift toward a ridge with a rotor beneath and behind it—a ridge that *almost* always has a boomer thermal working above it. Ahh…but, hope springs eternal in the human breast!

Landing

As we all know, what goes up must, eventually, come down, and in the case of aircraft, it's generally considered good form to bring them down in such a manner that they can be returned to the skies without repair, or worse: total rebuilding. This isn't as easy to accomplish as it might seem, and this fact isn't lost on the makers of CA adhesives and cellophane tape, which are the two most-often-used expedients of field repair. While landing is a rather simple task for the thermal soarer, owing to the large areas generally available for the purpose, such is seldom the case for the slope-soaring enthusiast. By their very nature, most slope-soaring sites tend to be quite rugged in their geological characteristics, frequently making it difficult to even find a landing site. The task of landing successfully is made even more difficult by the presence of wind, with the attendant shear, rotors, gusts and a myriad other atmospheric challenges.

In evaluating a landing site, keep in mind that the final goal is to land the glider *under control*, at the lowest possible ground speed, on the softest area available, and to keep it there until it can be retrieved. Keeping it there can be extremely difficult in a strong wind. Figure 7-8 depicts a traditional landing pattern—one that's preferred if a relatively large, flat area is available in the back of the lift-producing area of the slope. Here, the glider is flown downwind behind the rim of the slope (but not so far as to encounter the rotor), then turned into the wind to land, its ground speed being reduced by the strength of the wind.

This method usually results in a very soft, well-controlled landing, but there are a few "gotchas" to be aware of. Consider that the glider on downwind is coming toward the pilot at a high speed (its ground speed being

the sum of its air speed and the wind speed). Until they have considerable experience, most pilots find it difficult to control a glider that's flying toward them, and if control isn't precisely maintained on downwind, the glider can overshoot and fly into the rotor, or undershoot and fly back into the lift on final when headed into the wind. Timing is critical with this type of approach.

Another problem occurs when the pilot observes the glider's high ground speed at close range and, mistaking that ground speed for excessive air speed, attempts to slow the glider by pulling the nose up, thus increasing the wing's angle of attack. This tactic usually results in the glider stalling because its air speed is reduced below that necessary to sustain flight.

Still another consideration with this type of landing approach is that the top of the hill is usually cluttered with pilots, spectators, cars, etc., so a small error can cause *large* problems. Be sure to plan ahead and fly *precisely* and *safely*.

Many sites have insufficient suit-

able space for the traditional landing pattern, and a possible alternative is the cross-slope landing shown in Fig. 7-9. The strategy here is to fly the glider well down the slope to an area of light lift, then circle out and across the slope while bleeding off air speed and allowing the glider to be brought back up to the desired landing site by the slope lift. If the peanut butter and bread come out even, so to speak, the glider will stall at the same time as it reaches the landing site and will settle softly onto the slope. Obviously, this requires a very precise piloting technique and judgment, but then, we all have both, don't we? You bet!

The cross-slope landing is best performed with a glider equipped with ailerons, and it's least suitable for a glider with polyhedral upswept wing tips. This is because, to land at the optimum attitude, the glider will have to bank at the same angle as the slope. While this can be accomplished with a rudder/elevator-equipped glider, it's obviously much easier if ailerons are available.

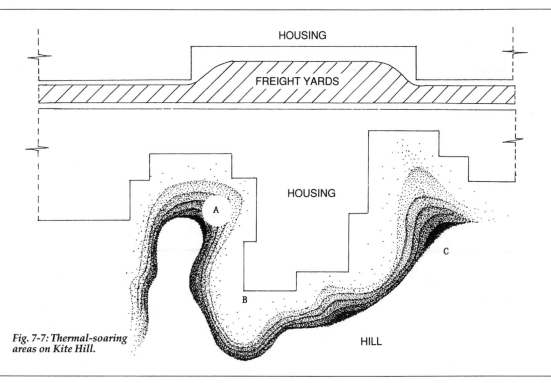

Fig. 7-7: Thermal-soaring areas on Kite Hill.

Another reason for the difficulty of landing a polyhedral glider using this method, is that it's quite likely that the wind will get under the upwind wing as the glider stalls and touches down, thus flipping it over onto its back and perhaps breaking a wing.

An excellent method of landing a polyhedral glider (or any glider) in a strong wind is to make a downwind full-stall landing against the slope, as shown in Fig. 7-10. As in the cross-slope landing just discussed, the glider is flown down and out from the slope to an area of light lift. It's then flown, at minimum controllable air speed, directly up the slope to the chosen landing site in such a way that it will stall and skid to a landing on reaching that site. This is a very safe landing technique in high winds since, once landed, the glider will be "pinned" to the slope by the force of the wind.

When using this type of landing approach, be aware that the glider's ground speed will be quite high when approaching and flying up the slope. Under these circumstances, it requires skill and experience to maintain minimum controllable air speed so as to precisely coordinate the timing of stall and touchdown.

Another thing to be careful of is the choice of a landing site. Obviously, this type of landing is out on a very steep or rocky slope, but the main thing to look out for is an absence of wing-grabbing objects in the touchdown area. If these are present, the probability of a cartwheel (either directly, owing to a wing catching, or the glider's turning sideways and allowing the wind to flip it) is very high. For the same reason, great care must be taken to keep the wings level until the glider is down and stationary, at which time you can rest assured that it's not going anywhere else; the wind will keep it there until you retrieve it!

If all else fails, or if you just feel like showing off, a final method of retrieving your glider is to catch it in your hand. The easiest way to do this is to "crab" the glider toward you across the slope at about waist height (maintaining minimum controllable air speed) and then fly it directly into your hand. You should catch the glider so that you wrap your hand around its nose with the wing butt resting on the web between your thumb and forefinger. This guarantees that the glider can't overshoot. And p*lease*, don't do this where others will be endangered, if you have a momentary lapse in your normally perfect glider-controlling capabilities!

Slope Contests

Most slope contests in the United States are local club affairs, because there aren't very many flying sites with sufficiently consistent wind and weather conditions to justify larger contests requiring long-term planning

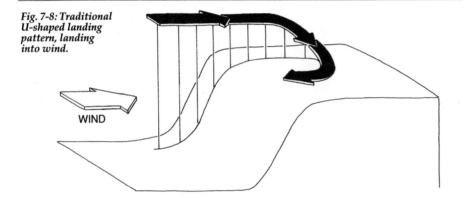

Fig. 7-8: Traditional U-shaped landing pattern, landing into wind.

WIND

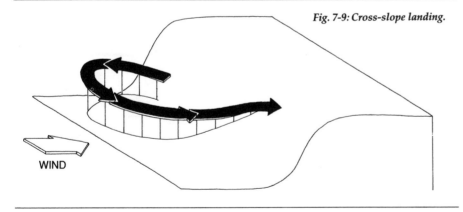

Fig. 7-9: Cross-slope landing.

WIND

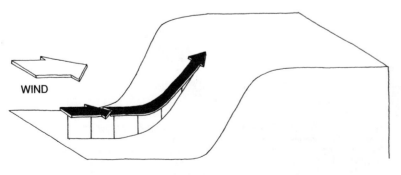

WIND

Fig. 7-10: Downwind up-slope landing.

Inverted flight, the joy of aerobatics.

and long-distance travel. This doesn't mean that the participants in these contests don't have a wonderful time, however! There are two basic types of competition flying: aerobatic contests and pylon racing.

● **Aerobatic Contests.** In most aerobatic contests, participants are handed sequence sheets depicting an aerobatic sequence using Aresti aerocryptographics (for details, read the chapter on aerobatics). The individual maneuvers are assigned "K," or difficulty, factors and then judged on a scale of 1 to ten. For instance, a hammerhead with a K factor of 25 and judged a score of 8, would net 200 points for the pilot performing it. The pilot with the highest point total for the sequence wins the contest.

The K factors, and the criteria for judging each maneuver, are generally the same as those specified in the Aresti Manual and the IAC Official Contest Rules, both of which are available from the International Aerobatic Club. The IAC is the governing body for full-scale contest aerobatics in the U.S., and it's a division of the Experimental Aircraft Association.

In a variation of this type of contest, each contestant creates his own sequence within a fixed overall K factor and then flies it. This is called a "free-style" competition.

● **Pylon Racing**. Pylon racing requires quite a bit more space and also more people than aerobatic contests; it's also a very exciting form of head-to-head competition.

To lay out a pylon race, a starting line is established and one pylon erected there, and another is placed at whatever seems to be a reasonable distance away that suits the flying sites: usually 100 yards, or so. Flag men are stationed at the far pylon, each equipped with a flag whose color is assigned to a particular glider. All pilots in a race launch

Accipiter makes a low pass.

their gliders simultaneously and head for the far pylon. Each flag man raises his flag as the glider assigned to him passes the pylon, at which point the pilot turns his glider around and races back to the starting line. Since it's difficult—if not impossible, with all the traffic—for the pilot to watch his glider and the flag man at the same time, a caller is assigned to each pilot to tell him when his flag has been raised. Generally, a complete race, or heat, if there are very many contestants, consists of 10 laps around the course.

An alternative start is the flying start, which begins with all the gliders airborne up-course of the starting line. The starter begins a 10-second countdown while the racers dive toward the starting line, hoping to cross it just as the countdown reaches zero. Any glider crossing the line early is either disqualified or required to make a 360-degree circle around the starting pylon before proceeding.

As you can see, there's a lot more to slope soaring than appears at first glance. It's a constantly challenging and rewarding activity that's pursued in an ever-changing, beautiful environment. And it's even more fun when combined with aerobatics, which is the subject of the next chapter.

A Talon makes a low-level pass.

Aerobatics

I've looked forward to writing this chapter, as aerobatic flying is my favorite glider flying activity (actually, I love performing aerobatics in full-scale aircraft, also)! Of course, the fact that I happen to live next to one of the best slope-soaring sites in Los Angeles that provides both slope lift and thermal activity may have

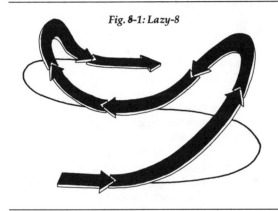

Fig. 8-1: Lazy-8

something to do with it! At any rate, aerobatics are fun! Big-time fun!

So what are aerobatics? The FAA (Federal Aviation Administration) defines aerobatic maneuvers as any maneuver that exceeds a bank angle of 60 degrees or a pitch angle of 30 degrees up or down, relative to the horizon. Well, according to that definition, you've probably already performed countless aerobatic maneuvers while learning to fly your glider! Now we're going to learn to perform those maneuvers intentionally and with precision!

Preparation and Safety

In order to perform aerobatics safely and predictably, you first need to be able to control the airplane well in normal flight. Practice flying the airplane both toward and away from you until your hand-eye coordination and recognition of the glider's direction are automatic. Practice making figure-8 turns in a fairly tight pattern. When you can execute these with

turns of even size on each end of the eight, without gaining or losing altitude in the turns, you're ready to start learning aerobatic maneuvers.

In the interest of safety, get the glider up to a fairly good altitude (three mistakes high is the usual rule) and well away from any spectators or anything expensive. Don't perform any maneuver close to the ground, people, or structures until you have thoroughly mastered it at altitude, and even then, stay away from people and anything you're not prepared to pay for! There's a reason pencils are made with erasers attached!

Wingovers and Lazy-8s

Your first aerobatic maneuver, the wingover, and its linked counterpart, the lazy-8 (Fig. 8-1), builds naturally from the figure-8 patterns you've already mastered. To perform a wingover, smoothly roll into a turn and pull back on the stick at the same time. Your goal is to achieve the maximum bank angle desired and maximum altitude possible at the 90-degree point of the turn, and then to smoothly roll out and descend to the original altitude at the original air speed, having completed a 180-degree turn. Linking two wingovers, one to the right and one to the left, results in a lazy-8.

While this sounds quite simple, it's really quite a complex and difficult maneuver to perform properly. The problem most people have is not raising the nose high enough at the start of the maneuver. This results in the glider's nose getting dragged across the horizon instead of soaring gracefully above it. Initially, it's important to use a lot of up-elevator, as it won't do much toward raising the nose once the glider passes 45-degrees of bank, or thereabouts. Remember, the glider should be just slightly above stall at the apogee of the turn. Coordinating the constantly changing roll and pitch inputs to achieve a smooth, evenly changing rate of climb and bank is extremely demanding, so don't get too discouraged if you don't catch on right away. Start with a bank angle of about 60-degrees at the top of the wingover, and gradually increase the angle until you can perform 90-degree knife-edge wingovers with impunity. Later, after you've practiced different types of rolls, try blending a roll into the apogee of the wingover. This is guaranteed to get everyone's attention, including yours!

Turns

Yes, there is such a thing as an aerobatic turn! To perform one, bank the glider sharply without allowing the nose to turn, then apply up-elevator to sweep the nose across the horizon, stopping the nose of the still-banked glider on the point desired, then roll smartly back to level flight. To qualify as an aerobatic turn, the bank angle must be between 60 and 90 degrees. Besides looking sharp, aerobatic turns make great crosswind correctors when included in sequences. I'll discuss that use in depth later in this chapter.

Spins

While the spin is a maneuver you've probably already encountered, either accidentally, or as a means of descending from thermal lift with

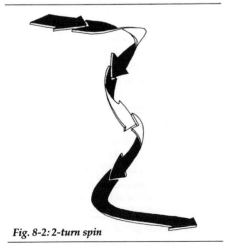

Fig. 8-2: 2-turn spin

minimum stress on the glider, it's also an aerobatic maneuver in its own right (Fig. 8-2). In this section, we'll discuss recovery from accidental spins (and in learning aerobatics you can be sure of many), as well as precision spins performed as aerobatic maneuvers.

Unintentional Spins. Regarding accidental spins, let's briefly review the conditions necessary for a glider to spin. First, the glider must stall: no stall, no spin. Second, the glider must be uncoordinated when it stalls; that is, there must be a destabilizing yaw (rudder), adverse yaw (aileron), or roll (aileron) input at the time of stall for the glider to spin. Third, the glider must remain stalled in order to continue spinning. Given these conditions, if the glider stalls with the stick back (up elevator), it will always enter an upright (inside) spin; if the glider stalls with the stick forward (down elevator), it will always enter an inverted (outside) spin. The reason we need to differentiate between upright and inverted spins is that recovery is different for each type of spin, and use of the incorrect recovery procedure will result in our worsening the spin instead of recovering. I should mention here that many gliders, especially the polyhedral types, can only be forced into an inverted spin with great difficulty, and even then will not remain in one for long, although they will remain stalled and tumbling. (Does that trigger your imagination regarding Lomcevaks, poly pilots?)

Since most gliders are inherently self-stabilizing, the first recovery method to try is simply releasing the controls and letting the glider recover from the spin on its own, although you'll have to recover from the remaining dive. If this doesn't work, then neutralize the ailerons, apply full rudder in the direction opposite the spin until rotation stops, then neutralize the rudder and apply down-elevator if

in an upright spin, or up-elevator if in an inverted spin, until the glider is flying again. If you don't have a rudder, neutralize the ailerons and use the elevator as just described. If neither of these methods works, then your glider will undoubtedly be reduced to kindling, and deservedly so. For its replacement, choose a better design and make sure the CG is where it belongs!

Precision Spins. In performing a spin as an aerobatic maneuver, think of it as having three parts: the entry, developed spin, and recovery. Ideally, the glider should enter a spin from level flight, the CG traveling in a straight line as the glider slows and the angle of attack increases to approach a stall. The nose and inside wing should fall through the horizon simultaneously as the spin develops. The glider should rotate the desired number of turns, then establish a vertical line before returning to level flight. So, let's have a shot at it.

To enter an upright spin, level the glider and ease the stick back to maintain level flight as it slows. As the glider nears the stall, ease the rudder in the direction of desired rotation and, as the resulting yaw stalls the inside wing, add full rudder while easing the stick full back as the nose drops. Don't use the ailerons, as they will flatten or steepen the spin, and don't relax full back pressure on the elevator, as this will accelerate the spin! Hold the controls in this position until ready to recover. For a one-turn spin, we'll probably have to lead our recovery by a quarter turn. Effect recovery by using full opposite rudder until rotation stops, then simultaneously neutralize the rudder and add down-elevator to establish a perfectly vertical down-line on the heading desired. Then use the elevator to return to level flight. The purpose of the vertical down line, besides looking nice, is to provide a method of controlling our speed for the next maneuver we wish to fly.

Loop

Since almost all aerobatic maneuvers, even the most complex, are made up of lines, loops, and rolls, we'll start by learning a basic loop (Fig. 8-3).

This maneuver is most easily performed at first with the glider going straight away from you and pointed into the wind. With the glider at a safe altitude, enter a shallow dive to about twice normal speed. Relax the forward stick pressure slightly to briefly return to level flight, then bring the stick straight back. As the glider nears the inverted position at the top of the loop, gradually release the back-pressure on the stick and let the glider float over the top, then, as

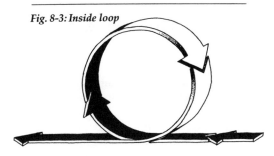

Fig. 8-3: Inside loop

the nose comes down, bring the stick straight back again to finish the loop at the same altitude as you started it. Because the glider is traveling faster than its trim speed, the nose will want to rise as you level off at the end of the loop. To prevent this, you'll have to maintain some forward pressure on the stick in order to maintain level flight while bleeding off the excess speed.

The most common error in performing the loop is pulling or pushing the stick to one side while pulling it back in the initial climb. This will invariably result in a crooked loop and flight path as the glider partially rolls around the loop. If you're absolutely certain that you're pulling straight back, yet the glider still wants to roll, or if you have to correct to one side to compensate for a rolling tendency, then your glider is out

of rig. Check the wing for warps, and especially check for equal wash-out at the wingtips. Make sure the horizontal stabilizer is perfectly aligned with the wing, and that the glider is properly balanced spanwise.

Once you're able to loop your glider in a straight path going away from you, start practicing with the model going at a right angle to your position. What you're working on now is making those loops nice and round, not pinched or flattened on top. When you have those loops looking as they should, try chaining them together. See how many you can do without losing flying speed. Try stacking them one on top of another. Experiment and have fun!

Aileron Roll

There are several different types of rolls, and the first one we'll learn is one I'll call an aileron, or victory, roll. These are easily performed with any glider having two control axes or more, although a rudder/elevator glider will fly a more barrel-shaped roll than one using ailerons.

Position your glider high and, with the glider heading away from you and into the wind, enter a shallow dive to about twice normal flying speed, then raise the nose to about a 30-degree angle above the horizon and hold it briefly at that angle. Now press the stick all the way to one side. As the glider rolls toward the inverted position, apply increasing forward pressure to the stick while continuing to hold it fully to one side. The purpose of the forward pressure is to keep the nose in place during the roll, and we'll need to decrease that pressure as the glider continues its roll toward upright. Release the side pressure just as the glider returns to a wings-level attitude. Now, level off and give yourself a pat on the back!

Make sure that you draw that short 30-degree line just before the start of the roll. If you start your roll while still holding back-pressure on the stick, you'll drive yourself crazy

trying to get a nice axial roll! The biggest problem in performing aileron rolls is coordination of the forward pressure with the glider's nose position. Bear in mind that, as the glider starts to roll, the nose will tend to turn in the direction of the roll. Use whatever forward pressure is necessary to keep the nose from veering away from the desired path; you'll need quite a bit! You may even have to adjust the glider's linkages for greater elevator throws.

Slow Roll

The aileron roll is as close as we'll be able to get to a slow roll with a 2-axis (rudder/elevator or aileron/elevator) glider, and the slow roll is the primary roll used in building more complex aerobatic maneuvers. So, to simulate a slow roll, we'll level off after the initial dive, instead of pulling up 30 degrees above the horizon. The glider's center of gravity should go in as straight a line as possible, resulting in a tight, axial roll. Practice this until you can make a level axial roll, while maintaining altitude and heading throughout the maneuver. Without full 3-axis controls, you won't be able to do it perfectly, but you sure can come pretty close!

If you have a 3-axis glider, your stick-work will be a little more complex, but you'll be able to fly a perfect slow roll! Remember, we've defined perfection as flying the glider in such a manner that the glider's center of gravity draws a perfectly straight line through the air. In order to do this, the glider must yaw slightly throughout the maneuver, in order to correct for the loss of lift in the knife-edge (90-degree) positions, while the elevator corrects for the effective wing incidence when inverted. Refer to the Fig. 8-4 in order to visualize the yaw corrections required to accomplish the slow roll.

Assuming your radio is set up for Mode II, your right thumb will perform exactly as it did for the aileron roll, but we're now going to add rud-

Fig. 8-4: Slow roll

der control with the left thumb. So, get set up "three mistakes high," dive to about twice normal flying speed, level the glider and briefly hold it there. Now start your roll as you did before, but this time as the glider reaches the 45-degree position or thereabouts, feed in rudder in the direction *opposite* the roll (left rudder when rolling right, or vice versa). Use whatever rudder deflection is necessary to hold the nose up and, as the glider rolls past the 90-degree point, start bringing it back to neutral. It should be neutral at about 135 degrees. As the roll progresses past inverted and nears 225 degrees, start feeding in rudder *with* the roll (right roll, right rudder or vice versa) to hold the nose up as the glider again approaches knife-edge. Past the 270-degree point, ease the rudder back to neutral and re-establish level flight.

If that sounds somewhat like patting your head and rubbing your stomach, just wait until you try it! Stick with it until you have it right, though; the slow roll is basic to many more complex maneuvers. As you improve, you may want to see just how slow you can get them. That will really sharpen your technique!

Dutch Rolls and Knife-Edge Flight (3-axis gliders only)

If you really have a lot of trouble educating that "dumb thumb," a good exercise is a series of Dutch rolls. These are really just a series of banks performed on a straight line to whatever degree of bank angle you wish. We'll start with 45-degree banks and progress to knife-edge.

Our goal is to bank the glider from side to side while proceeding in a straight line and holding a fixed altitude. To do this, set up and trim the glider slightly faster than normal flying speed in level flight. Bank the glider with ailerons, while holding the glider on a straight line with use of opposite rudder (right bank, left rudder, or vice versa) and elevator. Note that at steep bank angles, the elevator will correct for yaw (right/left), while the rudder will correct for pitch (up/down) deviations. As soon as you reach the desired degree of bank, immediately use ailerons to bank the glider in the opposite direc-

Fig. 8-5: Inside snap roll

tion. You'll need to increase the rudder pressure as you reverse the ailerons. Gradually relax it as the glider approaches a level attitude, then reverse rudder direction as the bank continues on the opposite side. As soon as you reach the desired bank angle, again reverse the ailerons, banking and correcting as before…and again…and again…ad nauseam.

This is a great coordination exercise and is quite difficult to do correctly. As you improve, keep increasing the bank angle until you can Dutch roll from 90 degrees to 90 degrees. When you can do this, stop at the 90-degree position and hold it there for a few seconds, increasing the rudder pressure as necessary to maintain altitude, then roll back level. Now do it the other way. Congratulations! You've just mastered knife-edge flight!

Lines, Inverted Flight

As mentioned earlier, the vast majority of complex aerobatic maneuvers are composed of lines, loops, and rolls. To complete our repertoire of basics, we need to learn to fly inverted.

There are two basic ways to attain inverted flight: by performing half a loop and leveling off inverted, or by performing half a roll and stopping inverted. The easiest way to gain a feel for inverted flight is from a loop, so start one with the glider coming downwind *toward* you and, as the glider reaches the top of the loop, use forward stick pressure to fly the glider inverted away from you and into the wind. You'll immediately notice that while the pitch inputs are reversed, with forward stick causing the glider to climb and back stick causing it to descend, the right and left roll inputs remain the same as in upright flight. When you're well out from the slope, or well upwind if flying from a flat site, either half loop or half roll to upright.

At this point, you may want to increase your glider's elevator throw. Sufficient down elevator is needed to be able to easily raise the nose and climb while inverted. Naturally, this inverted capability is going to vary considerably according to glider design. A polyhedral glider with a flat-bottomed airfoil isn't going to fly inverted as well or as long as a flying wing or a glider with a straight wing and a symmetrical airfoil, but it can be made to do surprisingly well. Make whatever adjustments you find necessary, then go back up and practice inverted level flight and turns, taking it easy at first and remaining well away from any obstacles.

When you can do nice, tight figure-8s while inverted, and transition smoothly from upright to inverted and back, you've got it mastered!

Hesitation Rolls

If you've read the information and practiced the maneuvers contained in the preceding section on inverted flight, you've already been doing two-point hesitation rolls! And if you've also read and practiced the sections on slow rolls and Dutch rolls, you have all the information and skills necessary to perform four-point rolls with ease! For those of you who haven't read and mastered the above, please do!

At this point, hesitation rolls will be a piece of cake! All you have to do is neutralize the roll (aileron) input at each point you wish to hesitate, while maintaining the other inputs. Try this first with two-point, then with four-point rolls; you'll find this far easier than you imagined! Fig. 8-4 shows the yaw angles required at each of the points of a four-point hesitation roll. For a bit of a challenge, try your hand at three, six, and eight-point rolls; that should keep you occupied for a while!

Snap Roll

The snap roll (Fig. 8-5) is a pretty violent maneuver and puts a lot of stress on the glider, so make sure your plane is strong enough and that you enter the maneuver at a relatively slow speed, or you really will snap it! Also, you'll need a rudder in order to snap roll your glider; it can't be done by ailerons and elevator alone.

Just as the spin, the snap roll is an autorotation maneuver, and it may be easier to understand it if you think of it as a forced spin in a horizontal plane. As in a spin, the glider must stall to enter a snap roll, and we accomplish this by a sharp rearward jab on the stick, and then

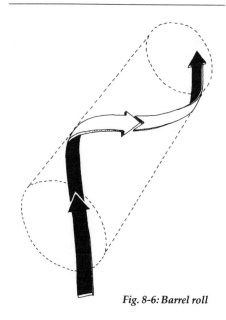

Fig. 8-6: Barrel roll

induce autorotation with an immediate application of full rudder in the desired direction. As we hold these inputs, the glider will enter and maintain a very rapid roll, which we'll stop by simply releasing the stick. If this recovery method doesn't work with your glider, use the same method you use for spin recovery to stop the roll.

Generally, it isn't necessary to apply full up-elevator to initiate the stall, and doing so will usually result in a mushy, yawing snap roll. It's often helpful to slightly relax the elevator back pressure once rotation has started; this will make the roll more axial and also faster. All of the above applies equally to outside snap rolls, except the maneuver is entered with sharp *forward* pressure on the stick, rather than backward.

Barrel Roll

There are at least five different ways to do barrel rolls. It seems each branch of the service has its own, but the one I'll teach you is the competition barrel roll (Fig. 8-6). This is a sort of loop and roll superimposed on each other, with the nose of the glider pointing 45-degrees off the original heading at the inverted mid-point of the maneuver.

To perform the barrel roll, dive for speed, then level the glider while flying directly away from you. Envision a point in the sky 45 degrees to the side of the glider's nose. Now, use elevator and ailerons (or rudder, or both) to climb and roll in such a manner that the glider will be at its highest point—about 20 degrees above the horizon, when inverted with its nose pointed at that spot. To accomplish this, you'll need to gradually relax the elevator back pressure while maintaining the roll input. Continue the roll and loop, gradually adding back pressure once again, to bring the glider back to level flight on the original heading. It's important to maintain a constant roll rate throughout the maneuver.

Split-S

The split-S (Fig. 8-7) combines a half-roll with a half-loop and is an excellent means of reversing direction while gaining speed for the next ma-

Fig. 8-7: Split-S

neuver. It does use up altitude in a hurry, though, so make sure you have plenty to spare!

To fly a split-S, establish level flight at a fairly slow speed, do a half slow roll and, just as the glider reaches the inverted position, ease the nose down into a half loop back to level flight. The points to watch in this maneuver are the transition from roll to loop, (there should be no straight line drawn here) and the looping portion, which should be a nice loop of even radius. Don't pinch the first part of the loop by applying too much back pressure too early.

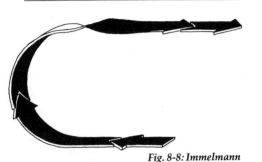

Fig. 8-8: Immelmann

Immelmann

The Immelmann is just the opposite of the split-S, that is, a half loop followed by a half roll (Fig. 8-8). The maneuver derives its name from the German aviator Max Immelmann, who used a similar maneuver during World War I to escape from, and subsequently get on the tail of, Allied aircraft. It's a good reversal maneuver, allowing a gain in altitude, as well as slowing the glider for entry to such slow speed maneuvers as snap rolls and spin entries.

To perform an Immelmann, dive to a speed slightly greater than normal looping speed, then pull up into a half loop. Upon reaching the top of the loop, immediately half-roll to upright, being careful not to draw a line between the loop and the roll. Because of the low speed, the glider will tend to sag a bit after the roll, so be sure to maintain sufficient back pressure to fly away straight and level.

Cuban 8

As mentioned earlier, most complete maneuvers are made up of the three basics: lines, loops, and rolls, and the Cuban 8 illustrates this well.

In full-scale aerobatic competition, only one-half Cuban 8s are flown, it being thought that adding the other half would be a needless duplication. Indeed, the half-Cuban (Fig. 8-9) is an especially useful maneuver for gliders, as it looks great and is a good way to reverse directions. We'll start with the half-Cuban, then put two together to make the full Cuban 8.

To start the half-Cuban, climb high and dive to the same speed you use for the loop, then level briefly, flying 90-degrees to your position so you can get a good look at the maneuver. Pull up and fly five-eighths of a loop just as you've done before but, as the nose reaches the 45-degree angle down, hold it there to draw a line. Now do half a slow roll to upright on that line, hold the 45-degree line for the same length as the previous one, and return to level flight. Easy, huh?!

Unfortunately, the full Cuban 8 (Fig. 8-10) isn't quite that easy; in fact it's downright difficult! The difficulty stems from the fact that a glider doesn't have an engine to pull it around the full maneuver. Instead, you have to utilize the energy stored in the dive, plus anything you can pick up along the way, to carry you around both looping segments. For this reason, if you're flying on a slope, it's best to plan the maneuver so that the second loop is performed close to the slope, in an area of maximum lift. If all else fails, it may be necessary to extend the first 45-degree down line in order to build up enough speed to make the second loop come out right.

Ideally, we should start the full Cuban 8 from level flight after gaining speed in the dive, but it will be much easier at first if we "cheat" a little while learning, by pulling up into the first loop directly from the dive. So, pull up into the loop, draw a 45-degree down line, half-roll, continue the line, and then pull up into a three-quarter loop for the second segment. If you have sufficient air speed to make it over the top with both loop segments the same size, you're almost home free; just draw another 45 down, half-roll, hold the line, then level off. That's all there is to the full Cuban 8!

Reverse Cuban 8

This is a more difficult maneuver to perform than the standard Cuban, because the half-roll is done while climbing, after which you must continue to climb inverted, thus bleeding off considerable speed before the looping portion (Fig. 8-11). As before, start with a reverse half-Cuban.

Unlike the standard half-Cuban, we can't "cheat" the entry as we did with the standard maneuver. So, dive to a blistering speed, level off briefly, then pull up to, and hold, a 45-degree line, do half a slow roll to inverted on that line, continue the line for the same distance as the first line, then ease the stick back to perform a five-eighths loop back to level flight. Got that?

The full reverse Cuban (Fig. 8-12) starts exactly the same way and continues into the looping portion, at which point we perform a three-quarter loop to a 45-degree up-line and proceed just as if we were flying a reverse half-Cuban, which, at this point, we are!

Fig. 8-9: Half Cuban

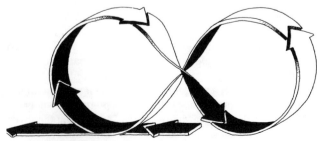

Fig. 8-10: Full Cuban-8

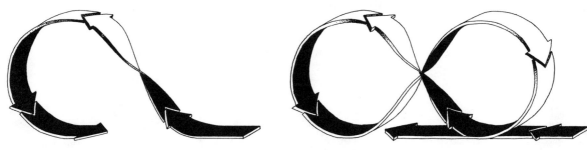

Fig. 8-11: Reverse half-Cuban

Fig. 8-12: Reverse Cuban-8

Laydown 8

As long as we're on the subject of figure 8s, we might as well initiate some outside maneuvers by learning to perform a laydown 8 (Fig. 8-13). This will be really simple if you have a glider with a symmetrical or semi-symmetrical airfoil, but it may be impossible for one equipped with a flat-bottomed or under-cambered airfoil.

To perform a laydown 8, begin as for a standard Cuban, looping up and over, and establish a 45-degree down line. Instead of rolling, however, hold the line to the entry point for the next looping portion, and use forward stick to push the nose up into a three-quarter outside loop. Draw the second 45-degree down line, and pull up to return to level flight.

Hammerhead

The hammerhead (Fig. 8-14) is a difficult maneuver to perform with a glider, as there is no propwash present to blow the tail around. As a result, gliders with three-axis controls

will have to "cheat" a little by leading the turnaround at the top with the rudder. Those without rudders will have to "cheat" for all they're worth to pull this one off!

Assuming you have a glider with three-axis controls, dive to gain some speed, then pull up into a perfectly vertical climb. As the glider slows while nearing the top of the maneuver, lead the turnaround by adding a little rudder, then, as the glider approaches the stall, but while it still has air moving over the control surfaces, punch in full rudder in the desired direction. As the glider pivots, use ailerons if and as necessary to correct any rolling tendency the glider may have. We want the glider to pivot evenly over the top and to establish a perfectly vertical downline on the exact opposite heading from which it entered the maneuver. A common error in the hammerhead is to fly over the top, caused by applying full rudder too soon. Precise timing is required to cause the glider to pivot within a horizontal distance of one-half wingspan—the desired

goal.

If your glider is one with only aileron and elevator controls, you will have to "cheat" the entry considerably in order to achieve a passable hammerhead. On the other hand, once you've set up the entry, you'll have a lot less work to do in completing the maneuver than a pilot using three-axis controls.

Our first "cheat" is one available only to those flying on a slope; we're going to use the lift blowing up the slope to assist the turnaround. The second "cheat" is to pull up with one wing slightly lower than the other if on a slope, that should be the wing pointing away from the slope and into the wind. So, dive *crosswind* for speed, and pull up to the vertical with the upwind wing slightly low by adding roll input during the pull-up. Now, wait. If you've set up the entry correctly, the glider will reach the top of its climb, stall, and rotate about its yaw axis. Simply stabilize the resulting dive on the opposite heading, return to level flight, and accept the compliments!

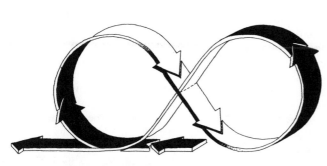

Fig. 8-13: Inside-outside laydown 8

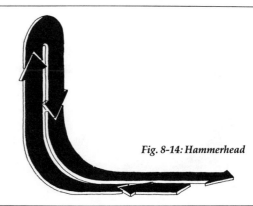

Fig. 8-14: Hammerhead

Fig. 8-15: Humpty-bump

Humpty Bump

Somewhat similar to a hammerhead, the humpty bump (Fig. 8-15) features a half loop instead of a pivot at the top, and always has at least a half roll on the upline. To perform this maneuver, you'll need to enter at considerable speed because of the vertical roll. Having attained sufficient speed, level briefly, then pull up to the vertical and draw a line, do a vertical half roll, continuing until the glider approaches the stall. Pull back on the stick so the glider does a tight half loop, then draw a vertical downline, pulling back to return to level flight at the bottom.

This is known as a pull, pull, pull humpty bump, as these are the elevator inputs used during the "plain Jane" version of the maneuver. Many other variations are possible and allow entries and exits in either upright or inverted flight, and exits in either the same or opposite direction as the entry. Try a pull, push, push version and you'll start to appreciate the versatility of this maneuver.

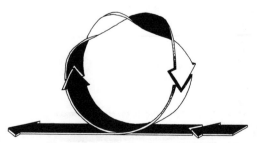

Fig. 8-16: Avalanche, slow roll on top

Avalanche

The avalanche is simply a loop with a roll on top (Fig. 8-16). Any type of roll will work fine, although, since the glider is traveling at a slow speed at the top of the loop, this is probably as good a place for a snap roll as any (Fig. 8-17). To perform the avalanche, enter a normal loop and, slightly before the glider reaches the inverted position, roll the airplane. It's important that the center of the roll be precisely in the middle of the loop, and that it continue the circumference of the circle. This is a loop with a roll at the top, not a half loop, roll, and half loop.

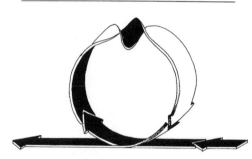

Fig. 8-17: Avalanche, snap roll on top

Square Loop

The square loop is an easy, yet impressive, maneuver (Fig. 8-18). To accomplish it, you'll need lots of speed as we pull up in a tight one-quarter loop from level flight. Draw a good vertical line, then pull into another one-quarter loop to inverted and draw a horizontal line the same length as the vertical line. Now pull into another quarter loop and draw a vertical downline the same length as the first two lines, then finish the maneuver with another quarter loop and return to level flight at the same altitude at which you started.

Interesting variations are six and eight-sided loops and, if you really want a challenge, try a three-sided loop!

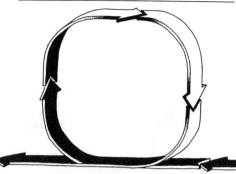

Fig. 8-18: Inside square loop

Other Maneuvers

If you've mastered the specific maneuvers outlined in this chapter, you should be able to fly any aerobatic maneuver your glider is capable of. Remember that almost all maneuvers are comprised of lines, loops, and rolls. Use your imagination to create new and interesting ones. You'll find that the variation is almost limitless! Here are some illustrations of a few of my favorites that work well for gliders. Figure 8-19 depicts an outside loop, which is performed by pushing the nose down from horizontal flight and continuing forward pressure as necessary throughout the maneuver. When only a half loop is performed, the maneuver is called an English bunt. In either case, be sure to begin the maneuver at a slow enough air speed so that the airframe will not be overstressed as the glider gains speed in the dive

Figures 8-20 and 8-21 show two types of vertical S's, one plain outside-inside type, and the other outside-outside with a half-roll in between. Other variations start with a half-roll to inverted, or incorporate a full roll in the middle. I'm sure you'll come up with your own favorites. Again, it's necessary to start these maneuvers from a relatively low air speed, as considerable speed will be gained in the diving portion of the half-loops. For an interesting challenge, start at the bottom and perform the S's while climbing.

The number of maneuvers that can be assembled from the basic components, lines, loops, and rolls is limited only by your imagination and the capabilities of you and your glider, of course. Go back over the maneuvers in this chapter and think about different ways you can combine them to make up new ones, then have some fun by going out and flying them. You'll be amazed at how fast your flying improves!

Sequences

As soon as you've mastered the basics of aerobatics and a few of the maneuvers that incorporate them, you'll want to assemble those maneuvers into sequences of continuous aerobatics; continuous as long as you have altitude and air speed, that is. In performing aerobatic sequences with gliders, energy management is critical. And where does this energy come from?—altitude and air speed. We can trade altitude for air speed by diving, or we can trade air speed for altitude by climbing, but there's a lot to this, because a glider is always sinking in relation to the air around it. Therefore, we need to plan our sequences in such a manner that the maneuvers complement each other in terms of entry and exit speed, and altitude loss or gain.

For instance, we'll usually start each sequence with a screaming dive which provides lots of air speed for, say, a humpty bump. Since the exit from the humpty is fast, let's use that air speed to gain altitude with an Immelmann, which leaves our glider high and slow. Here's a perfect place for a snap roll, which can then be fol-

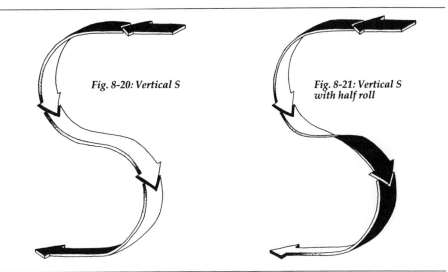

Fig. 8-20: Vertical S

Fig. 8-21: Vertical S with half roll

lowed by a spin, with its slow entry and fast exit. Coming out of the spin, a loop would fit nicely, perhaps followed by a hammerhead, then a slow roll, etc.

Notice that the above sequence not only provides for compatible speeds and altitudes for the maneuvers, but also for reversals of direction. This is done not only to keep the maneuvers directly in front for best viewing, but also to keep the glider in the area of maximum lift if flying from a slope. In this way, you can achieve the maximum time for your sequence before having to break to climb to altitude once again.

The Aresti System of Aerocryptographics

As you have learned, the key to developing and flying good sequences is planning, and as you plan your sequences you'll need a way to record them for future reference. The preferred way to do this is to use the Aresti system of aerocryptographics, a method of notating aerobatics devised by Count Jose Luis Aresti, and adopted by all major aerobatic organizations. The full Aresti system is far too voluminous to be included here, filling 182 pages in the official Aresti Manual. For full-scale competition purposes, as of January 1, 1989, the Aresti Manual will be replaced by

the FAI Aerobatic Catalog that will incorporate the Mueller system. For model aerobatic purposes, the differences between the two systems are insignificant and, in most cases, nonexistent. For those who are interested, either manual may be obtained from the International Aerobatic Club, P. 0. Box 3086, Oshkosh, WI 54903-3086. For sport-flying purposes, however, possession of these manuals is totally unnecessary, and can be confusing. Those elements of the system useful to us are outlined in the next few paragraphs. Referring to Figs. 8-22 and 8-23, you'll notice that all maneuvers start and end with level flight, the start of each maneuver being shown by a dot, and the end by a short vertical line. Upright flight is denoted by a solid line, inverted flight by a dashed line, and knife-edge flight by alternating dots and dashes. Inside snaps and spins are depicted using hollow triangles with a "tail" in the direction of travel, while outside versions of those maneuvers use solid triangles, also equipped with "tails."

For flight and judging purposes, maneuvers flown in front of the observer from right to left, or vice-versa, are flown on the X-axis, while maneuvers flown toward and away from the observer are on the Y-axis. The Aresti system differentiates between maneuvers which begin and/or end on the X or Y-axis by depicting

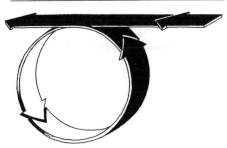

Fig. 8-19: Outside loop, starting with English bunt

Fig. 8-22: Aresti aerocryptographics

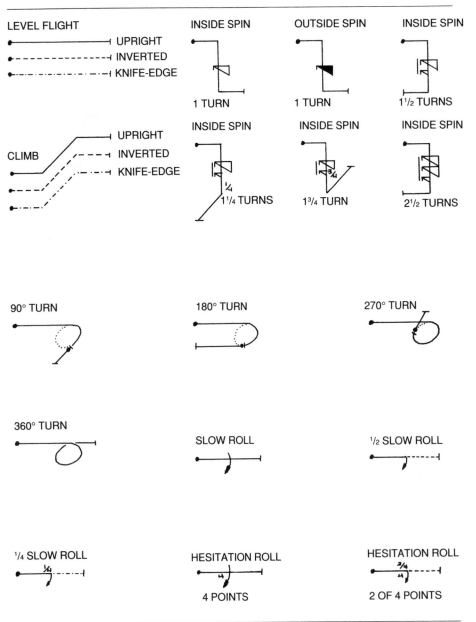

specified. An arrow pointing to a circle depicts a barrel roll. While most maneuvers are pretty much flown as depicted, an exception is the reverse half-Cuban, as shown in Fig. 8-23. Here, the 3/4 looping portion is drawn with a 90-degree angle at the bottom to enable it to be readily differentiated from a standard half-Cuban. The above information, combined with careful study of Figs. 8-22 and 8-23, should provide all the information you'll need to put the Aresti system to work for you.

Of course, the whole purpose of aerocryptographics is to enable the uniform composition, preservation, communication, and performance of aerobatic maneuvers and, most important sequences. A sample aerobatic sequence is shown in Fig. 8-24 and, yes, it can be performed nonstop by a good R/C glider and pilot, given sufficient altitude and/or a slope that is working well. This sequence illustrates several features essential to the composition of a "good" sequence. To begin with, the sequence is well-balanced, that is, the maneuvers are evenly divided between right, left, and center, with interesting turn-around maneuvers being utilized to keep the glider moving back and forth across the slope (or area in front of the pilot, if thermalling). Further, the exit and entry speeds of the maneuvers are compatible and allow for a smooth transition from one to the next.

In our example, the exit speed from the loop (1) is a good entry speed for the following slow roll (2), and the exit speed from that will work just fine for entering the hammerhead (3). On the downline of the hammerhead, we can establish any speed we want, and we'll want plenty to smoke across the flying area and trade our air speed for altitude with an Immelmann (4). We'll be slow coming out of the Immelmann—just what we need for the snap roll (5) and subsequent 1 1/2-turn spin (6). As we draw the vertical line after the spin, we can gain all the speed neces-

those on the Y-axis with a 45-degree line starting and/or ending the maneuver. This can be seen by the aerocryptograms of the 1 1/4 and 1 3/4 turn spins and the 90- and 270-degree turns in Fig. 8-22. Remember that the 45-degree line at the start and/or end of each maneuver represents flight on the Y-axis only. Each maneuver *always* begins and ends in level flight.

Slow rolls (axial, not necessarily slow in rate of rotation) are drawn using an arrow curving in the direction of flight. If the arrow passes through the line of flight, it denotes a full roll; if it butts against the line of flight, then it denotes a half-roll, unless a fraction appears next to it indicating other partial rolls. A whole number appearing next to the arrow means that a full hesitation roll of that many points is to be performed, while a fraction combined with the whole number designates a partial hesitation roll of the number of points

Fig. 8-23: Aresti aerocryptographics

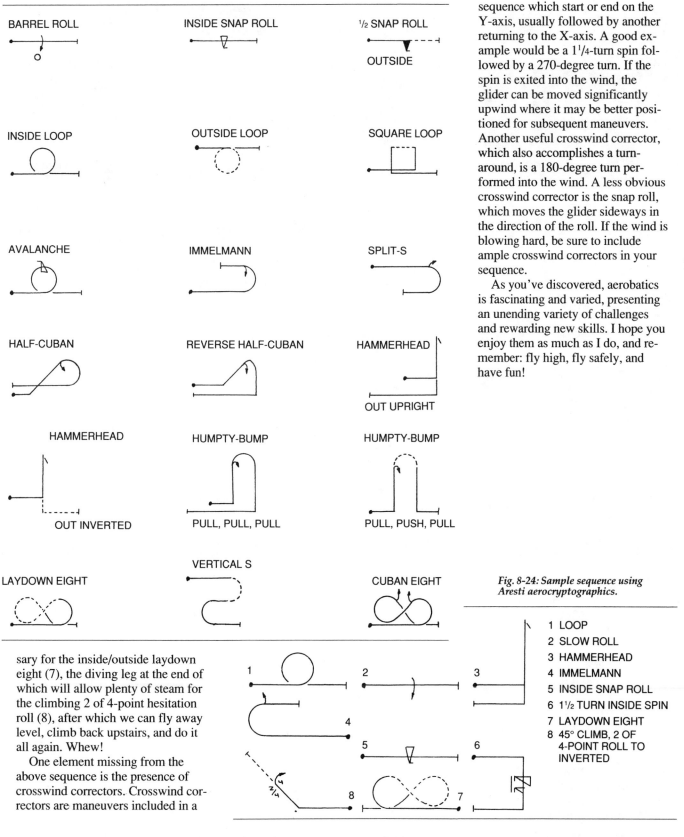

BARREL ROLL

INSIDE SNAP ROLL

½ SNAP ROLL

OUTSIDE

INSIDE LOOP

OUTSIDE LOOP

SQUARE LOOP

AVALANCHE

IMMELMANN

SPLIT-S

HALF-CUBAN

REVERSE HALF-CUBAN

HAMMERHEAD

OUT UPRIGHT

HAMMERHEAD

HUMPTY-BUMP

HUMPTY-BUMP

OUT INVERTED

PULL, PULL, PULL

PULL, PUSH, PULL

VERTICAL S

LAYDOWN EIGHT

CUBAN EIGHT

sequence which start or end on the Y-axis, usually followed by another returning to the X-axis. A good example would be a 1¼-turn spin followed by a 270-degree turn. If the spin is exited into the wind, the glider can be moved significantly upwind where it may be better positioned for subsequent maneuvers. Another useful crosswind corrector, which also accomplishes a turn-around, is a 180-degree turn performed into the wind. A less obvious crosswind corrector is the snap roll, which moves the glider sideways in the direction of the roll. If the wind is blowing hard, be sure to include ample crosswind correctors in your sequence.

As you've discovered, aerobatics is fascinating and varied, presenting an unending variety of challenges and rewarding new skills. I hope you enjoy them as much as I do, and remember: fly high, fly safely, and have fun!

sary for the inside/outside laydown eight (7), the diving leg at the end of which will allow plenty of steam for the climbing 2 of 4-point hesitation roll (8), after which we can fly away level, climb back upstairs, and do it all again. Whew!

One element missing from the above sequence is the presence of crosswind correctors. Crosswind correctors are maneuvers included in a

Fig. 8-24: Sample sequence using Aresti aerocryptographics.

1 LOOP
2 SLOW ROLL
3 HAMMERHEAD
4 IMMELMANN
5 INSIDE SNAP ROLL
6 1½ TURN INSIDE SPIN
7 LAYDOWN EIGHT
8 45° CLIMB, 2 OF 4-POINT ROLL TO INVERTED

A Final Note from the Editor

Why does anyone write a book? Why spend interminable hours at the keyboard tapping out a message to the world? It's obvious that the love of soaring was the inspiration that motivated Mr. Gornick to put all this information together. We hope that his great enthusiasm for the sport is conveyed here and that you're encouraged to try your hand at this silent, but exciting, sport.

There's enough information here to help you choose your equipment wisely and to fly it safely. You should be able to buy a radio and to find a thermal; to check the washout and adjust the ballast. But don't try to remember everything at once in a frantic rush to soar. Glider people work as quietly and efficiently as our creations that sweep the sky. Here's a list of the addresses that the author thought might be helpful, but other companies also produce and sell glider products. Have fun!

Rich Uravitch

Ace R/C Inc., 116 W. 19 St., Box 511C, Higginsville, MO 64037.
Airtronics, Inc., 11 Autry, Irvine, CA 92718.
American Sailplane Designs, 2626 Coronado Ave., No. 89, San Diego, CA 92154.
Astro Flight, 13311 Beach Ave., Marina Del Rey, CA 90292.
Bob Martin R/C Models, 1520C Acoma Ln., Lake Havasu City, AZ 86403.
Buzz Waltz RC Designs, 3390 Paseo Barbara, Palm Springs, CA 92262.
California Soaring Products, P.O. Box 367, Topanga, CA 90290.
Carl Goldberg Models, 4734 West Chicago Ave., Chicago, IL 60651.
Combat Models, 2128 48th Court, San Bernardino, CA 92407.
Craft Air (division of Dynaflite)
Davey Systems Corp., One Wood Lane, Malvern, PA 19355.
Dodgson Designs, 21230 Damson Rd., Bothell, WA 98021.
Dynaflite, 1578 Osage, San Marcos, CA 92069.
Futaba Corporation of America, 4 Studebaker, Irvine, CA 92718.
GM Precision Products, 510 E. Arrow Hwy., San Dimas, CA 91773.
Hobby Lobby International, 5614 Franklin Pike Circle, P.O. Box 285, Brentwood, TN 37027.
Hobby Shack, 18480 Bandilier Circle, Fountain Valley, CA 92728.
House of Balsa, 20130 State Rd., Cerritos, CA 90701.
International Aerobatic Club, P.O. Box 3086, Oshkosh, WI 54903.
Larry Hargrave Models, c/o Robin's Hobby Service, 1844 W. Glendaks Blvd., Glendale, CA 891201.
Larry Jolly Model Products, 5501 W. Como, Santa Ana, CA 92703.
League of Silent Flight, P.O. Box 39068, Chicago, IL 60639.
Midway Model Co., P.O. Box 9, Midway City, CA 92655.
Off the Ground Models, Inc., 606C West Anthony Dr., Urbana, IL 61801. (now available from Ace R/C)
Pierce Aero, available from Mutchler's Hobbies, Inc., 4620 Crandall-Lanesville Rd., Corydon, IN 47112.
Robbe Model Sport, 180 Township Line Rd., Belle Mead, NJ 08502.
Sig Manufacturing Co., 401 S. Front St., Montezuma, IA 50171.
Top Flite Models, 2635 S. Wabash Ave., Chicago, IL 60616.
Tower Hobbies, P.O. Box 778, Dept. MAN, Champaign, IL 61824.
United Model Products, 301 Holbrook Dr., Wheeling, IL 60090

Informative Modeling

Model Four-Stroke Engines by the renowned model-engine expert, Peter Chinn, covers the history, design, development and operation of the ever-popular four-stroke engine. This profusely illustrated book will answer all your engine questions and it covers all the four-stroke engines, including opposed twins, radials, wankels and conventionals, plus a gallery of all the latest four-strokes now available. This is the definitive four-stroke engine book, which any modeler will enjoy. **$13.95**

Advanced Radio Control Car Modeling by Rich Hemstreet and the editors of *Radio Control Car Action* is the most up-to-date and informative book on radio-control car modeling and racing. It covers the whole spectrum of R/C cars—everything from ¹/₂₄- to ¼-scale, plus the new ¹/₁₀-scale stock cars. You'll find advanced information on race strategy, modifications, handling, gearing, tires, R/C electronics, two-stroke engines, airbrushing Lexan, and much more. There's a wealth of useful information in this book, and it will answer many of your most difficult questions. It's a great book, which no R/C car enthusiast should be without. **$9.99**

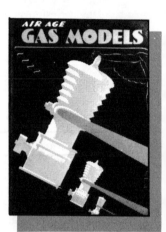

Scale Aircraft Drawings, Vol. I, World War I from the editors of *Model Airplane News*, contains incredibly detailed scale drawings, historical data and rare photos of popular World War I aircraft. Everything from the Wright Flyer to the Fokker D. VIII is covered. The drawings are from master aviation illustrators, such as Wylam, Nye, Nieto, Karlstrom and others. These three-views will make any modeling or aviation buff's heart palpitate. This high-quality book is invaluable to scale modelers or anyone who loves aircraft and would make a great gift for the aviation enthusiast in your life! Two more volumes are planned for the near future. **$12.95**

Gas Models is a true collector's book. From the early editors of *Model Airplane News*, it contains the best of modeling from the '30s and '40s, including great technical info and classic construction articles from that Golden Age period. If you're interested in modeling's roots, take a ride back in time with this vintage work. You'll love the nostalgic photos! **$7.95**

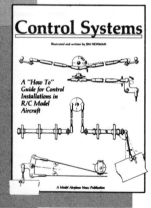

Control Systems by the master hobby illustrator, Jim Newman, is a treatise on installing more complex control systems in R/C aircraft. It's great for new installations or modifying your present flying machine. The illustrations are impeccable. You'll definitely want this book for your R/C library. **$4.95**

---

400 Great R/C Modeling Tips by Jim Newman contains a tremendous wealth of modeling tips for the radio-control enthusiast. There are numerous time- and money-saving tips on building, tools, engines, covering, controls, landing gear, the flight box and much more—all beautifully illustrated by the master, Jim Newman. These tips have been picked from the ever-popular "Hints & Kinks" column featured in *Model Airplane News* for over a decade. They're the innovative ideas of hundreds of modelers. This is one book the active radio-control modeling enthusiast should have in his workshop and it's also great for the beginner. **$9.95**

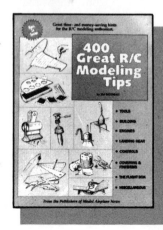

Available at your local hobby shop or order direct.

Books Air Age Book Mart

form and entertain any modeling buff.

Basics of Radio-Control Helicopters by Paul Tradelius is the most comprehensive up-to-date book on radio-control helicopters. It will provide answers to every important question for all R/C helicopter enthusiasts. From selecting the "right" helicopter kit and radio, through building the machine, and right up to aerobatic flying, internationally recognized expert Paul Tradelius takes you through it all. Helicopter theory is presented in terms you can really understand. Autorotation, collective pitch, gyro stabilization and other helicopter terms are all clearly explained. What kind of tools you'll need, how to accomplish the inevitable repairs, even where to buy—it's all here. **$9.95**

Basics of Radio Control Cars by Doug Pratt and the editors of *Radio Control Car Action* magazine is the newest and most informative book on the exploding R/C car hobby. This profusely illustrated book includes information on all scales of gas and electric cars, plus building tips, modifications, R/C electronics, chargers, racing, track designs, maintenance and much more. It's a great book for the beginner R/C car enthusiast and would make a fantastic gift. **$9.99**

Giant Steps is the definitive source for information on giant radio-control aircraft. Written by the editors of *Model Airplane News*, it covers virtually every facet of building, flying, accessories, engines, electronics, radio and covering. Experts discuss everything from basic materials to sophisticated landing gear. Even if you're not into giant-scale planes, this book contains a wealth of modeling information and is loaded with great photos. **SOLD OUT** **$12.95**

Basics of Radio Control Boat Modeling—from John Finch and the editors of *American Boat Modeler* comes the most informative book on radio-control boat modeling and racing. It covers the entire spectrum of R/C power boats, including deep-vees, hydros, monos and tunnels, in both gas and the hot new electrics. You'll find in-depth information on R/C electronics, wiring, servos, batteries, two-stroke engines, cooling systems, carburetors, speed controllers, hull nomenclature, drive systems, propellers, hardware setups, stuffing box, struts and bearings, trimming, balancing, timing, racing classes and much more—plus a wealth of useful modeling and racing tips! There are hundreds of photographs and many illustrations. A tremendous modeling resource. No R/C boat enthusiast should be without it! **$9.95**

Model Airplane News Plans Directory—If you're into scratch-building, or want to try your hand at it, there are more airplane plans in this catalog than anywhere else. Giant scale, pattern, warbirds, sport ships, trainers, bipes, jets—the list is seemingly endless, and there is definitely one for you to build. Who knows? You might be the next Scale Masters champion! This catalog also contains a listing of the fabulous Wylam, Nye, Nieto and Larson scale drawings published in *Model Airplane News* over the years. **$2.00**

Books make great gifts!